MW00899837

MyBatis in Practice

A Step by Step Approach for Learning MyBatis Framework

Prepared by

Srinivas Mudunuri

Trademarks

Trademarked names may appear in this book. Trademarks and product names used in this book are the property of their respective trademark holders. The author of this book is not affiliated with any of the entities holding those trademarks that may be used in this book.

Oracle, MyBatis and Java are registered trademarks of Oracle and/or its affiliates. Other names may be trademarks of their respective owners.

Cover Design & Images By: Richard Castillo (http://www.digitizedchaos.com)

Printing History:

July 2013   First Print

ISBN-10: 1491003014

ISBN-13: 978-1491003015

Dedicated

To

My Mother
&
Son Abhishek

Table of Contents

Preface

This document provides a step-by-step approach for developing applications using MyBatis framework. It is specially designed to help the individuals who want to learn MyBatis framework. This book can be used as a reference table guide for MyBatis and Java developers.

The Audience for this book is:

- Individuals who want to learn the complete use of MyBatis framework.
- Individuals who are looking for step-by-step approach for developing applications using MyBatis framework.
- Individuals who want to learn transaction management using MyBatis.
- Individuals who want to learn Spring-MyBatis.
- Individuals who want to learn MyBatis-Velocity.
- Individuals who want to learn MyBatis-provided annotations.
- Individuals who want to learn MyBatis support for executing database stored procedures and functions.
- Architects who want to compare the technical capabilities of various open-source data access frameworks.

A prior knowledge of Java and SQL programming is required. It is good to have some XML knowledge but an XML novice can understand without much difficulty. A prior knowledge of database programming is essential. It is also good to have Spring framework knowledge but it is not mandatory. This book is designed for intermediate and advanced Java developers. The chapters are arranged based on the increasing order of their complexity and its dependency. Inline code snippets are provided while explaining each topic and a complete working example is provided at the end of the each topic. A step-by-step approach is followed for developing code examples, so it is easy for a beginner to understand the application development.

The topics covered in this book are given below:

- Introduction to MyBatis
- Database Operations (CRUD)
- MyBatis Annotations
- MyBatis - Executing Stored Procedures and Functions
- MyBatis-Spring Transaction Management
- MyBatis with Velocity
- Migrating from iBatis to MyBatis

This book covers the MyBatis framework-related technology standards such as introduction to MyBatis, MyBatis support for executing select, insert, delete, and update statements, MyBatis-provided annotations, MyBatis support for executing stored procedures and functions, MyBatis integration with Spring, MyBatis integration with Velocity, MyBatis-Spring support for transaction management, and migration from iBatis to MyBatis. A step-by-step approach is followed throughout and this book contains approximately 50 Java programs for a better understanding of the topics.

Structure of the Book

This book contains 7 chapters. The structure of the book is given below.

Chapter 1 (Introduction to MyBatis) covers the introduction to MyBatis framework and its evolution. This chapter also covers the MyBatis terminology, MyBatis configurations, database set-up configurations, MyBatis advantages, and its architecture.

Chapter 2 (Database Operations-CRUD) covers the required MyBatis integration with Spring framework, MyBatis and Spring configurations, executing select, insert, delete, and update statements using core MyBatis, executing select, insert, delete, and update statements using MyBatis-Spring, building and executing dynamic SQL statements, working with sequence numbers and retrieval of auto-generated sequence numbers using MyBatis framework. It also covers the complete MyBatis API and its use with code examples.

Chapter 3 (MyBatis Annotations) covers the MyBatis support for annotations, the various ways of executing select, insert, delete, and update statements using MyBatis annotations, working with sequence numbers and retrieval of auto-generated sequence numbers using MyBatis annotations.

Chapter 4 (MyBatis-Executing Stored Procedures and Functions) provide the details about MyBatis support for executing database stored procedures and functions, XML-based approach for executing stored procedures and functions, Annotation-based approach for executing stored procedures and functions, the use of IN, OUT, and CURSOR parameters while executing the database stored procedures and functions.

Chapter 5 (MyBatis-Spring Transaction Management) provide the details about MyBatis-Spring declarative transaction management, programmatic transaction management, and annotation-based transaction management.

Chapter 6 (MyBatis with Velocity) will help you to understand the Velocity syntax and fundamentals, MyBatis integration with Velocity, Velocity syntax for generating SQL statements, and building dynamic SQL statements using MyBatis-Velocity.

Chapter 7 (Migrating from iBatis to MyBatis) provides the details of migration from iBatis to MyBatis, and MyBatis support for logging information using open-source frameworks.

Code Examples – Code examples are provided for each topic. It will help you to develop the code; step-by-step instructions are provided for developing the code examples.

About the Author

Srinivas earned his master's degree in Machine Design Engineering from Roorkee-IIT, India. He is a Sun Certified Java Programmer (SCJP), Sun Certified Java Developer (SCJD), Sun Certified Enterprise Architect (SCEA), Sun Certified Business Component Developer (SCBCD), Sun Certified Developer for Java Web Services (SCDJWS), Bea Weblogic Certified Enterprise Developer and an Open Group Certified TOGAF-9 Practitioner. Srinivas has been working with Java related technologies since its very early days. He has over 14 years of experience in developing the enterprise applications using Spring, Web Services, and Java EE-related technologies.

Srinivas is currently working as a senior Java developer and TOGAF practitioner in Phoenix, Arizona. He is an active member in various Java user forums and he is a regular speaker in Java user groups. Srinivas is a technology evangelist and he teaches Spring, Web Services, and Java EE-related technologies during his free time. He is the author of following books.

- Imbibing Java Web Services – A Step by Step Approach for Learning Java Web Services.
- Spring Framework – A Step by Step Approach for Learning Spring Framework.
- MyBatis in Practice – A Step by Step Approach for Learning MyBatis Framework.

Acknowledgements

This book could not have been written without the encouragements, supports and contributions from many people.

The primary references to this book are Java Specification Requests (JSR's), various MyBatis articles, white papers, tutorials available on the web, my own experience with MyBatis framework. I would like to thank everyone who contributed to the Java and MyBatis community which I used to gain the knowledge of Java and MyBatis technologies.

First of all, I would like to thank my friend Uday Thota who helped me to build my career in USA. The sad part is he is no more with us; may Almighty God grant him eternal rest and may his soul rest in peace.

I would like to thank my friend Purna Katrapati; who helped me while doing master's thesis using C programming language and Surfer package. I would say he was my first teacher helped me to start my programming career. I would like to thank another friend Kishori Sharan; who trained me in Oracle and Power Builder technologies. This book would not have completed without Kishori's help and guidance. He is there to help me all the time, time after time and every time.

I would like to thank Richard Castillo who designed the cover page for this book.

I would like to thank Weidong Zhang who was my lead Architect in my previous job; he gave me an opportunity to implement MyBatis for a student learning application. It helped me to gain in-depth practical knowledge in MyBatis which I used later in several applications.

I would like to thank my colleagues Darr Moore, Himanshu Mandalia, Vivek Sharma, Venkata Srinivas Tripasuri, and Suk Fung. At present I am working with them; thanks to everyone who helps me at work place every day and it is a great team.

I would like thank my friends Rama Raju Saripella, Prabhakar Kandikonda, Gopi Krishnam Raju Sangaraju, Vijay Polasani, Madhava Rao, Ramesh masa, Raghavendra Swamy, Ravi Nallakukkala, Suresh Pattipati, Neeraj Oberai, Rakesh Jaiswal, Tej Kalidindi, Ranga Anne, Rama Chitirala, Madhan Retnaswamy, Ramesh Kondru, Bala Talagadadeevi, Phani Narem and Phani Tangirala. I would say simple thanks are not enough for their help and support. A special thanks to Madhan who helped me during my initial days of stay in Phoenix, Arizona.

I would like to thank all my students who provided me an opportunity to teach Java and Web Services.

A special thanks to Sylburn Peterkin, Narayan Sithemsetti, Gopinath Kakarla, and Mallik Somepalli who helped me to review this book in spite of their busy schedules.

I would like to thank my childhood class mates Tulasi Narayana Rao, Venkata Appa Rao, Srinivas Baratam, and Siva Kumar. I have spent so much time with them and I do carry lot of childhood memories. Once in a while, I go to my home town they are always there to give a helping hand and warm reception.

Finally, I want to thank my wife Radha Mudunuri, my mother, father, brothers and in-laws who provide me great support and help all the time. I would like to thank my four year old son Aayush and ten months old daughter Akshara; she has just started speaking a few words and she always want to play with her cousin sister, Aakanksha.

Source Code, Questions and Comments

Please direct all your questions and comments to mudunuri1234@yahoo.com

Chapter 1. Introduction to MyBatis

Java Database Connectivity (JDBC) is a Java-based data access technology used for accessing the relational databases and is part of Java EE. JDBC is also called Core-JDBC. Sun released the first version of JDBC in 1997. Later on, several open-source and proprietary data access frameworks were developed that provide a higher-level API for data access. The commonly used open-source data access frameworks currently available on the market are listed below.

- Core-JDBC
- Spring-JDBC
- Hibernate
- MyBatis
- Java Persistence API (JPA)
- Java Data Objects (JDO)
- TopLink

Spring-JDBC is the technology used for accessing relational databases. Spring hides the low-level details of the Core-JDBC and provides several high-level template classes for executing SQL statements. Spring-JDBC takes care of low-level details such as opening a connection, closing a connection, closing a ResultSet, statements execution, exception handling, transaction management, ResultSet iteration, and so forth.

Hibernate is an object-relational (OR) mapping framework used for accessing relational databases. Hibernate maps the domain object classes to the database tables and provides a hibernate query language (HQL) for working with domain objects. Hibernate runtime converts the HQL to SQL for executing SQL statements.

MyBatis is a ResultSet-Object mapping framework used for accessing relational databases. MyBatis was formerly known as iBatis and does the opposite of what the hibernate framework does. MyBatis hides the low-level details of the Core-JDBC and provides several high-level utility classes for mapping the ResultSet data to the domain object classes.

All of the preceding frameworks provide the same functionality using different techniques; all are used for accessing the databases. The Spring framework can be integrated with all the above-listed frameworks. This book illustrates the complete use of MyBatis framework.

In general, the data access frameworks are categorized as follows:

- Data access frameworks that provide high-level API's for accessing the ResultSet data (Spring-JDBC).
- Data access frameworks that use the object-relational (OR) mapping technique (Hibernate, JPA, TopLink, etc.)
- Data access frameworks that use the ResultSet-object mapping technique (MyBatis)

This chapter will discuss the following topics:

- MyBatis introduction
- MyBatis configurations and database set-up instructions
- MyBatis terminology
- How to execute select, insert, delete, and update statements using MyBatis

- MyBatis advantages
- MyBatis architecture

The phrase MyBatis has been extremely popular in the JDBC world for several years. Enterprise applications have been using the MyBatis framework for more than a decade. It is an open-source data persistence framework for Java and .Net platforms. *Clinton Begin* invented this framework in 2001, and it was released under the Apache license. The completely redesigned and renamed project MyBatis-3.0 was released in 2010. This project was moved out from the Apache license in 2010.

MyBatis is a unique framework that provides a ResultSet-object mapping technique for accessing the relational databases. The database returned result sets are mapped directly to the application domain objects. MyBatis provides a simple and more flexible programming model for accessing the databases. MyBatis supports the following programming models:

- XML-based programming model
- Annotation-based programming model
- Combined programming model (XML and Annotations)

XML-based programming model: In this approach, the SQL queries and MyBatis-specific configurations, and metadata are specified in XML files. MyBatis API uses this information for executing SQL statements.

Annotation-based programming model: In this approach, the SQL queries and MyBatis-specific configurations, and metadata are specified using Java API. MyBatis provides Java API for executing SQL statements. The XML configurations can be completely eliminated in this approach.

Combined programming model (XML and Annotations): In this approach, the SQL queries and MyBatis-specific configurations, and metadata are specified in XML and Java classes. Some of these configurations are specified in XML and the rest is specified using MyBatis API.

This book illustrates all of the above specified programming models. Also, MyBatis can be easily integrated with the following frameworks.

- MyBatis integration with Spring and Google Guice
- MyBatis-Velocity integration

MyBatis Integration with Spring and Google Guice: In this approach, the Spring and Guice-provided dependency injection and inversion of control features can be used with MyBatis. Spring provides a high-level template class, which uses different methods to execute select, insert, delete, and update statements.

MyBatis-Velocity integration: In this approach, the Velocity scripting language can be used for generating the SQL queries and dynamic SQL statements.

This book illustrates the complete use of Spring and Velocity integration with MyBatis framework.

Advantages of MyBatis

This section illustrates the technical and non-technical benefits of the MyBatis framework.

- Uses the power of SQL statements, easy to execute complex sub-queries, and correlated sub-queries.
- Simple, flexible, easy to learn, simpler in package size, and provides more powerful features for building dynamic SQL statements.
- MyBatis provides support for XML and Annotation-based programming model.
- MyBatis provides plug-ins for integrating with Spring, Google Guice, and Velocity frameworks.
- Simplified programming model compared to Core JDBC.
- MyBatis provides support for managing transactions. MyBatis can take advantage of Spring transaction management to support the Aspect and Annotation-based programming models.
- The complete project is available in a single JAR file.
- MyBatis provides a simplified approach for migrating from iBatis to MyBatis.
- MyBatis is a preferred solution if you need more control over SQL statements.

MyBatis Architecture

Figure 1-1 illustrates the MyBatis architecture.

Figure 1-1 MyBatis Architecture

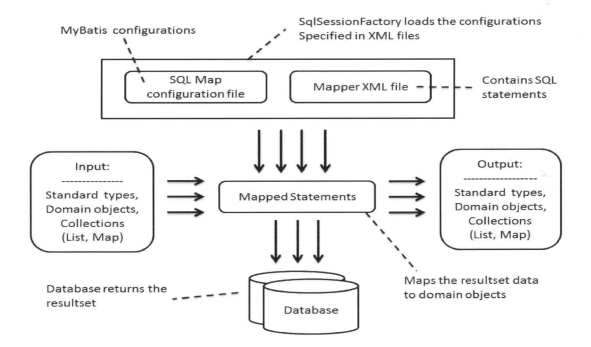

The following points illustrate the MyBatis artifacts and components as shown in Figure 1-1.

- All SQL queries are specified in MyBatis mapper XML files. This file contains SQL statements such as select, insert, delete, update, and so forth.
- SQL Map configuration file has configuration settings such as MyBatis-specific settings, domain objects, mapper XML files, data source information, and so forth.
- Mapped statements execute the SQL statements and map the ResultSet data to domain objects.
- Mapped statements can take any valid Java type as input and provide the valid Java type as output.

Prerequisites/Setting Up the Environment

The following list of JAR files is required for developing MyBatis-Spring code examples:

- mybatis-3.x.jar
- mybatis-spring-1.0.0-RC3.jar

The following list of JAR files is required for developing MyBatis-Velocity code examples:

- mybatis-velocity-1.0.jar
- velocity-1.7.jar

Download the MySQL server-specific driver class files. The JAR file name is provided below.

- mysql-connector-java-5.1.6-bin.jar

Download the Oracle server-specific driver class files. The JAR file name is provided below.

- ojdbc.jar

The following table has the complete list of JAR files required to develop code examples provided in this chapter.

aopalliance-1.0.jar	asm-4.1.jar
aspectjrt.jar	aspectjtools-1.5.4.jar
aspectjweaver.jar	cglib-nodep-2.2.2.jar
commons-beanutils.jar	commons-codec-1.4.jar
commons-collections.jar	commons-configuration.jar
commons-dbcp-1.2.1.jar	commons-digester.jar
commons-discovery.jar	commons-el.jar
commons-io-1.2.jar	commons-lang-2.3.jar
commons-logging.jar	commons-validator.jar
mybatis-3.2.2.jar	mybatis-spring-1.2.0.jar
mybatis-velocity-1.0.jar	mysql-connector-java-5.1.6-bin.jar
ojdbc14.jar	org.springframework.aop-3.0.7.RELEASE.jar
org.springframework.asm-3.0.7.RELEASE.jar	org.springframework.aspects-3.0.7.RELEASE.jar
org.springframework.beans-3.0.7.RELEASE.jar	org.springframework.context.support-3.0.7.RELEASE.jar
org.springframework.context-3.0.7.RELEASE.jar	org.springframework.core-3.0.7.RELEASE.jar
org.springframework.expression-3.0.7.RELEASE.jar	org.springframework.jdbc-3.0.7.RELEASE.jar
org.springframework.orm-3.0.7.RELEASE.jar	org.springframework.transaction-3.0.7.RELEASE.jar
velocity-1.7.jar	

Database Configuration Settings

The examples provided in this book are tested with Oracle and MySQL databases. MySQL is an open-source relational database. This section will help you to create the required tables, stored procedures, and functions.

Oracle Installation and Database Setup

The Oracle database can be used to demonstrate the code examples provided in this chapter. Follow the below-provided instructions to install the Oracle database.

- Download the Oracle database express edition from the oracle web site. Oracle provides the "OracleXE.exe" installer for Windows.
- Use the following credentials:
  - Password = password
  - Default user-name = SYSTEM
  - Default port = 8080 (You can change this)
- After completing the installation → Go to All Programs → Oracle database express edition → Go to database homepage.
- The database login page will be displayed → enter user name and password → this one take you to the Oracle administration page → here you can create your own database schema and tables.
- Create tables, database stored procedures, and functions in the created database schema.

The following database tables are created. The "pet" table definition is provided below.

```
CREATE TABLE SPOWNER.PET (
    ID NUMBER(5,0) NOT NULL,
    NAME VARCHAR2(75),
    OWNER VARCHAR2(75),
    SPECIES VARCHAR2(75),
    SEX CHAR(1),
    BIRTH DATE,
    DEATH DATE,
    CONSTRAINT PET_ID_PK PRIMARY KEY (ID)
    USING INDEX
)
/
```

Create a sequence number. This sequence number is used as a primary key column in the "pet" table.

```
CREATE SEQUENCE SPOWNER.PET_ID_SEQ
    START WITH 1
    MAXVALUE 99999999999999999999
    MINVALUE 1
    NOCYCLE
    CACHE 20
    NOORDER
/
```

Insert the following data into the "pet" table. Use the following SQL statements.

```
INSERT INTO PET VALUES (SPOWNER.PET_ID_SEQ.nextval,
            'Puffball','Diane','hamster','f', sysdate, NULL);

INSERT INTO PET VALUES (SPOWNER.PET_ID_SEQ.nextval, 'Fluffy',
            'Harold','cat','f', sysdate, NULL);

INSERT INTO PET VALUES (SPOWNER.PET_ID_SEQ.nextval, 'Slim',
            'Dennis','snake','f', sysdate, NULL);
```

Create the following stored procedures. The "read_pet" stored procedure code is provided below.

```
CREATE OR REPLACE PROCEDURE spowner.read_pet(in_name IN VARCHAR2,
    out_owner OUT VARCHAR2,
    out_species OUT VARCHAR2,
    out_sex OUT VARCHAR2,
    out_birth OUT DATE,
    out_death OUT DATE)
IS
BEGIN
    SELECT owner, species, sex, birth, death
    INTO out_owner, out_species, out_sex, out_birth, out_death
    FROM spowner.pet
    WHERE name = in_name;
END;
/
```

The following commands are used to execute the stored procedure.

```
DECLARE
    out_owner VARCHAR2(100);
    out_species VARCHAR2(100);
    out_sex VARCHAR2(100);
    out_birth DATE;
    out_death DATE;
BEGIN
    spowner.read_pet('Slimmy', out_owner, out_species, out_sex,
                out_birth, out_death);

    DBMS_OUTPUT.PUT_LINE('out_owner :  ' || out_owner);
    DBMS_OUTPUT.PUT_LINE('out_species :  ' || out_species);
    DBMS_OUTPUT.PUT_LINE('out_sex :  ' || out_sex);
    DBMS_OUTPUT.PUT_LINE('out_birth :  ' || out_birth);
    DBMS_OUTPUT.PUT_LINE('out_death :  ' || out_death);
END;
/
```

The "read_all_pets" stored procedure code is provided below. This stored procedure returns an Oracle CURSOR.

```
CREATE OR REPLACE PROCEDURE spowner.read_all_pets(
        c_allpets OUT SYS_REFCURSOR)
IS
BEGIN
    OPEN c_allpets FOR
    SELECT name, owner, species, sex, birth, death FROM spowner.pet;
END;
```

/

Create the following stored function. The "`get_pet_owner`" stored function code is provided below.

```
CREATE OR REPLACE FUNCTION spowner.get_pet_owner(in_name IN VARCHAR2)
RETURN VARCHAR2 IS
    out_owner VARCHAR2(200);
BEGIN
    SELECT owner
    INTO out_owner
    FROM spowner.pet where name = in_name;

    RETURN out_owner;
END;
/
```

MySQL Installation and Database Setup

The MySQL database can used to demonstrate the code examples provided in this chapter. MySQL is an open-source relational database. Follow the instructions provided below to install the MySQL database.

- Download the MySQL installer from the "http://dev.mysql.com/downloads/mysql/" web-site. MySQL provides the "mysql-5.5.28-winx64.msi" installer for Windows.
- Use the following credentials:
  - Password = mysql
  - Default user-name = "root"
  - Default port = 3306
- After completing the installation → Go to All Programs → Open MySQL Command Line Client
- Execute the following commands from the MySQL command line client.
  - Show all available databases → SHOW DATABASES;
  - Use the test database → USE TEST;
  - Show all available tables in test database → SHOW TABLES;
- Create tables, database stored procedures, and functions in the TEST database.

The following database tables are created. The "pet" table definition is provided below.

```
CREATE TABLE pet (name VARCHAR(20),
    id MEDIUMINT NOT NULL AUTO_INCREMENT,
    owner VARCHAR(20),
    species VARCHAR(20),
    sex CHAR(1), birth DATE, death DATE,
    PRIMARY KEY (id)
);
```

The "USER" table definition is provided below.

```
CREATE TABLE USER (
    id MEDIUMINT NOT NULL AUTO_INCREMENT,
    first_name CHAR(30) NULL,
    last_name CHAR(30) NULL,
    PRIMARY KEY (id)
```

```
) ENGINE=MyISAM;
```

Create the following stored procedures. The "read_pet" stored procedure code is provided below.

```
DELIMITER //
CREATE PROCEDURE read_pet (
    IN in_name VARCHAR(100),
    OUT out_owner VARCHAR(100),
    OUT out_species VARCHAR(100),
    OUT out_sex VARCHAR(100),
    OUT out_birth DATE,
    OUT out_death DATE)
BEGIN
    SELECT owner, species, sex, birth, death
    INTO out_owner, out_species, out_sex, out_birth, out_death
    FROM pet where name = in_name;
END //
DELIMITER;
```

The following commands are used to execute the stored procedure.

```
CALL read_pet('Fluffy', @out_owner, @out_species, @out_sex, @out_birth,
@out_death);
```

Use the following command to view the stored procedure output.

```
SELECT @out_owner, @out_species, @out_sex, @out_birth, @out_death;
```

The "read_all_pets" stored procedure code is provided below. This stored procedure returns a ResultSet.

```
DELIMITER //
CREATE PROCEDURE read_all_pets()
BEGIN
    SELECT name, owner, species, sex, birth, death FROM pet;
END //
DELIMITER;
```

The following command is used to execute the stored procedure.

```
CALL read_all_pets();
```

Create the following stored function. The "get_pet_owner" stored function code is provided below.

```
DELIMITER $$
CREATE FUNCTION get_pet_owner(in_name VARCHAR(200)) RETURNS VARCHAR(200)
BEGIN
    DECLARE out_owner VARCHAR(200);

    SELECT owner
    INTO out_owner
    FROM pet where name = in_name;
```

```
        RETURN out_owner;
END;
$$
```

The following command is used to execute the stored function.

```
SELECT get_pet_owner('Fluffy') AS owner; $$
```

MyBatis Terminology

This section explains the terminology commonly used in MyBatis framework while developing Java applications. MyBatis framework terminology is defined below.

SqlSession: This is the primary MyBatis-provided API class used to select, insert, delete, and update operations. This class has the following methods.

- selectOne(…)
- selectList(…)
- selectMap(…)
- insert(…)
- update(…)
- delete(…)
- commit(…)
- rollback(…)
- getConnection(…)
- getConfiguration(…)
- close(…)

SqlSessionFactory: This class is used to load the MyBatis configuration files. The `openSession(...)` method of the `SqlSessionFactory` class is used to create an instance of `SqlSession` class.

The following code demonstrates the relation between `SqlSession` and `SqlSessionFactory`.

```
private static SqlSession getSqlSession() throws Exception {
    String resource = "core-mybatis-config.xml";
    InputStream inputStream = Resources.getResourceAsStream(resource);
    SqlSessionFactory sqlSessionFactory = new
                SqlSessionFactoryBuilder().build(inputStream);

    // Obtains the SqlSession
    return sqlSessionFactory.openSession();
}
```

SqlSessionTemplate: This is the core class used in MyBatis-Spring for executing SQL statements such as select, insert, delete, and update, as well as stored procedures and functions. The `SqlSessionTemplate` class is obtained by injecting the `SqlSessionFactory` reference. An example of a `SqlSessionTemplate` configuration is provided below.

```
<bean id="sqlSessionFactory"
    class="org.mybatis.spring.SqlSessionFactoryBean">
```

```
                    <property name="dataSource" ref="dataSource"/>
                    <property name="configLocation" value="sqlMapConfig.xml" />
</bean>

<bean id="sqlSessionTemplate"
        class="org.mybatis.spring.SqlSessionTemplate">
        <constructor-arg index="0" ref="sqlSessionFactory"/>
</bean>
```

SQL Mapper File: This file contains `<select>`, `<insert>`, `<delete>`, and `<update>` XML tags used for executing SQL statements.

MyBatis Configuration File: This file contains configurations such as MyBatis framework-specific settings, domain object configuration, data source information, mapper XML files, and so forth.

Spring Application Context File: This file is used only if you use MyBatis with Spring. This file contains configurations such as data source information, `SqlSessionTemplate`, `SqlSessionFactory`, transaction manager, application-specific DAO classes, and so forth.

MyBatis Configuration Settings

This section illustrates the required configuration settings and artifacts to execute SQL statements. MyBatis can be used with and without the Spring framework.

MyBatis

In this approach, the required configuration files are listed below.

- mybatis-config.xml
- mapper.xml

The "mybatis-config.xml" file contains configurations such as MyBatis-specific settings, domain object configuration, data source information, mapper XML files, and so forth.

The "mapper.xml" file is used to specify the SQL statements such as select, insert, delete, update, and so forth.

Chapter -2 provides the complete structure of these files in greater detail.

MyBatis-Spring

In this approach, the required configuration files are listed below.

- mybatis-config.xml
- mapper.xml
- applicationContext.xml

The "mybatis-config.xml" file contains configurations such as MyBatis-specific settings, domain object configuration, mapper XML files, and so forth.

The "mapper.xml" file is used to specify the SQL statements such as select, insert, delete, update, and so forth.

The "applicationContext.xml" file contains configurations such as data source information, transaction manager, spring SQL session template, application-specific DAO classes, and so forth.

Chapter -2 provides the complete structure of these files in greater detail.

Obtaining the Database Connection

How to obtain a database connection is illustrated in this section. This section provides the details of database connection using Core-JDBC, MyBatis, and MyBatis-Spring.

Core JDBC

In this approach, the core-JDBC provided API is used to establish a connection to the database. The execute(...) and executeUpdate(...) methods of the Statement class is used for executing SQL statements. Developers can use this low-level API to execute SQL statements, iterate the ResultSet data, and populate the domain objects.

The following Java code is used to obtain a database connection for executing SQL statements.

```
private static Statement getConnection() throws Exception {
    Class.forName("oracle.jdbc.OracleDriver");
    Connection con = DriverManager.
    getConnection("jdbc:oracle:thin:@localhost:1521:xe",
                "SPOWNER", "PASSWORD");
    Statement stmt = con.createStatement();
    return stmt;
}
```

MyBatis

MyBatis hides the low-level details of the database connection, provides a high-level API for executing SQL statements, and maps the ResultSet data to domain objects. The selectList(...), insert(...), and update(...) methods of the SqlSession class is used to execute the SQL statements and map the ResultSet data to domain object classes.

The following Java code is used to obtain a database connection for executing SQL statements. The SqlSession class encapsulates the ResultSet to domain object mapping details.

```
private static SqlSession getSqlSession() throws Exception {
    String resource = "core-mybatis-config.xml";
    InputStream inputStream = Resources.getResourceAsStream(resource);
    SqlSessionFactory sqlSessionFactory =
            new SqlSessionFactoryBuilder().build(inputStream);
    return sqlSessionFactory.openSession();
```

```
}
```

MyBatis-Spring

In this approach, `SqlSessionTemplate` class encapsulates `SqlSessionFactory`, which is used to establish the database connection. The `SqlSessionTemplate` class is used for executing SQL statements and maps the ResultSet data to domain object classes.

The following XML code is used to obtain a database connection for executing SQL statements.

```xml
<bean id="sqlSessionFactory"
    class="org.mybatis.spring.SqlSessionFactoryBean">
    <property name="dataSource" ref="dataSource"/>
    <property name="configLocation" value="sqlMapConfig.xml"/>
</bean>

<bean id="sqlSessionTemplate"
    class="org.mybatis.spring.SqlSessionTemplate">
    <constructor-arg index="0" ref="sqlSessionFactory"/>
</bean>
```

SQL Statements Syntax

This section illustrates the fundamentals of MyBatis SQL mapping statements.

XML -based

In this approach, the SQL statements are defined in mapper XML files. An example select statement configuration is provided below.

```xml
<select id="getPetObject"
        parameterType="java.lang.String"
        resultType="PetDVO">
    SELECT ID as id, NAME as name, OWNER as owner,
        SPECIES as species, SEX as sex,
        BIRTH as birth, DEATH as death
    FROM Pet WHERE name = #{name}
</select>
```

Let us review the SQL statement.

- select → used for executing the select statements
- id → unique name used for identifying the SQL statement.
- parameterType → input parameter type
- resultType → ResultSet return type mapping object.
- NAME, OWNER etc. → represents the database table column names.
- name, owner, etc. (column alias names) → represents domain object properties

MyBatis maps the database's returned ResultSet to the domain objects. The Java code used to retrieve the matching pet is provided below.

```
PetDVO petDVO = sqlSessionTemplate.selectOne("getPetObject", inputMap);
```

Similarly, the following XML element is used for update statement.

```xml
<update id="updatePetData" parameterType="java.util.Map">
    UPDATE Pet p SET p.birth = #{birth}, p.sex = #{sex}
    WHERE p.name = #{name}
</update>
```

The following XML element is used for delete statement.

```xml
<delete id="deletePet" parameterType="java.util.Map">
    DELETE FROM Pet WHERE name = #{name} AND species = #{species}
</delete>
```

The following XML element is used for insert statement.

```xml
<insert id="insertUser" parameterType="java.util.Map"
        useGeneratedKeys="true" keyProperty="id">
    INSERT INTO Pet (ID, NAME, OWNER, SPECIES, SEX, BIRTH)
    VALUES (#{id}, #{name}, #{owner}, #{species}, #{sex}, #{birth})
</insert>
```

An example `<select>` statement definition and its supported attributes are provided below.

```xml
<select id="selectPerson"
    parameterType="java.lang.String"
    resultMap="petResultMap"
    resultType="hashmap"
    flushCache="false"
    useCache="true"
    timeout="5000"
    fetchSize="100"
    statementType="PREPARED"
    resultSetType="FORWARD_ONLY">
```

Let us review the significance of each attribute.

- id → a unique identifier used for each SQL statement.
- parameterType → the data type of the input parameter that is passed into the statement.
- resultMap → an externally defined reference data type.
- resultType → the data type of the statement output parameter. Either `resultMap` or `resultType` is used in `<select>` statement.
- flushCache → flushes the cache whenever statement is executed.
- useCache → the statement results are cached.
- timeout → waiting time for the database to respond to a request before throwing an exception.
- fetchSize → ResultSet batch size.
- statementType → the valid types are STATEMENT, PREPARED, and CALLABLE.
- resultSetType → the driver dependent attribute.

An example `<insert>` statement definition and its supported attributes are provided below. If your database supports auto-generated keys, you can insert the auto-generated key value as follows:

```
<insert id="insertUser"
        parameterType="java.util.Map"
        useGeneratedKeys="true"
        keyProperty="id"
        flushCache="true"
        statementType="PREPARED"
        timeout="20">
    INSERT INTO User (first_name, last_name)
    VALUES (#{firstName}, #{lastName})
</insert>
```

Alternatively, use the following approach if your database does not support the auto-generated keys.

```
<insert id="createPet" parameterType="java.util.Map">
    <selectKey keyProperty="id" resultType="int" order="BEFORE">
        SELECT PET_ID_SEQ.nextval AS id FROM dual
    </selectKey>

    INSERT INTO Pet (ID, NAME, OWNER, SPECIES, SEX, BIRTH)
    VALUES (#{id}, #{name}, #{owner}, #{species}, #{sex}, #{birth})
</insert>
```

An example `<update>` statement definition and its supported attributes are provided below.

```
<update id="updatePetData"
        parameterType="java.util.Map"
        flushCache="true"
        statementType="PREPARED"
        timeout="20">
    UPDATE Pet p
    SET p.birth = #{birth}, p.sex = #{sex}
    WHERE p.name = #{name}
</update>
```

An example `<delete>` statement definition and its supported attributes are provided below.

```
<delete id="deletePet"
        parameterType="java.util.Map"
        flushCache="true"
        statementType="PREPARED"
        timeout="20">
    DELETE FROM Pet WHERE name = #{name} AND species = #{species}
</delete>
```

More details of the above-specified XML statements are provided in Chapter -2.

Annotation -based

MyBatis provides annotations such as `@Select`, `@Update`, `@Insert`, and `@Delete` and so forth. In this approach, these annotations are used at method level to execute the SQL statements. An example "select" statement definition is provided below.

```
@Select(" SELECT ID as id, NAME as name, OWNER as owner, " +
           " SPECIES as species, SEX as sex, BIRTH as birth, " +
           " DEATH as death " +
         " FROM Pet where name = #{name} ")
public PetDVO getPetObject(String petName);
```

An example "delete" statement definition is provided below.

```
@Delete("DELETE FROM Pet WHERE name = #{name} AND species = #{species}")
public void deletePet(PetDVO petDVO);
```

An example "update" statement definition is provided below.

```
@Update(" UPDATE Pet SET birth = #{birth}, " +
         " sex = #{sex} WHERE name = #{name} ")
public void updateData(@Pram("birth")Date birth,
                       @Param("sex")String sex,
                       @Param("name")String name);
```

Similarly, an example "insert" statement definition is provided below.

```
@Insert(" INSERT INTO Pet (ID, NAME, OWNER, SPECIES, SEX, BIRTH) " +
         " VALUES (#{id}, #{name}, #{owner}, #{species}, #{sex}, #{birth})")
@Options(useGeneratedKeys = true, keyProperty = "id")
public void insertPetData(PetDVO petDVO);
```

Comparison between Object-Relational (OR) Mapping and MyBatis

The following table summarizes the comparison between the various technical features of OR mapping frameworks (Hibernate, JPA, Toplink, etc.) and MyBatis.

OR Mapping Frameworks	MyBatis
This is an object-relational mapping technique used to access the databases. The domain objects are mapped to database entities.	MyBatis is a ResultSet-Object mapping technique used to access the databases. The ResultSet data maps to the domain objects. This is the reverse of what Hibernate does.
Preferable for simpler database schemas and tables that have well defined relationships.	Uses the power of SQL statements, easy to execute complex sub-queries and correlated sub-queries.
Requires a steeper learning curve; tuning and debugging are challenging.	Simple, flexible, easy to learn, simpler in package size, and provides more powerful features for building dynamic SQL statements.
Developers use QL (query language) to define relationships and join conditions. OR	Developers use SQL statements for database operations.

mapping framework runtime converts the QL to SQL for database interaction. QL is similar to SQL.	
QL is database independent.	SQL is database dependent. It is the preferred solution if you need more control over SQL statements.

Summary

This section summarizes the features provided by the MyBatis framework. Figure 1-2 summarizes the most important points described in this chapter.

- The `SqlSession` class is the primary MyBatis-provided API class used to select, insert, delete, and update operations.
- The `SqlSessionTemplate` class is the core class used in MyBatis-Spring for executing SQL statements such as select, insert, delete, and update, as well as stored procedures and functions.
- The required MyBatis configurations, database settings, and artifacts are discussed.
- MyBatis provides XML and Annotation-based approaches for executing SQL statements.

Figure 1-2 MyBatis introduction.

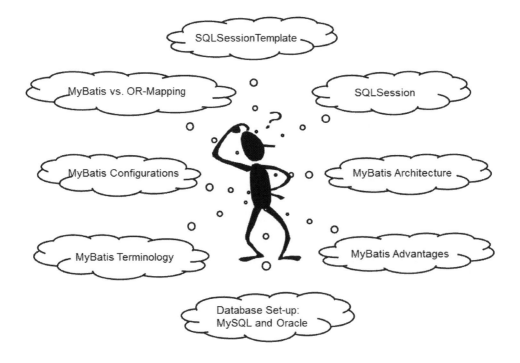

Chapter 2. Database Operations (CRUD)

MyBatis-3.0 supports both XML and annotation-based approaches for building and executing the SQL statements. This chapter illustrates the XML-based approach for executing select, insert, update, and delete statements. In the XML-based approach, the required MyBatis configuration settings and SQL mapping statements are specified in XML files. In general, the commonly used configurations such as datasource information, environment settings, data transfer objects, and SQL mapping files are specified in XML files. MyBatis runtime uses the configurations specified in XML while executing the SQL statements.

This chapter will discuss the following topics:

- The required MyBatis and Spring configurations
- Spring integration with MyBatis
- Executing select, Insert, delete, and update statements using Core MyBatis
- Executing select, Insert, delete, and update statements using MyBatis with Spring
- The various ways of executing select, insert, update, and delete statements using MyBatis
- Building and execution of dynamic SQL statements
- Working with sequence numbers
- Retrieval of auto-generated sequence numbers using MyBatis

Prerequisite and Configuration Settings

This section illustrates the configurations required for MyBatis (Core) and MyBatis with Spring.

- Make sure "Pet" table is created before executing the code examples.
- Make sure "id" sequence number is generated if you work with Oracle database. Refer to Chapter -1 for details.
- Make sure "User" table is created before executing the code examples.

MyBatis (Core)

The following files are used to specify the MyBatis-specific configurations and SQL queries. It is not mandatory to use a specific file name; use any meaningful name. Let us review the purpose of each file in this section.

1. Mapper.xml
2. SqlMapConfig.xml

Mapper.xml → this file contains database-specific SQL statements such as select, insert, delete, and update. The structure of the "mapper.xml" file is provided below.

```
<?xml version="1.0" encoding="UTF-8" ?>
<!DOCTYPE mapper PUBLIC "-//mybatis.org//DTD Mapper 3.0//EN"
                "http://mybatis.org/dtd/mybatis-3-mapper.dtd">
```

```
<mapper namespace="petmapper">

    <select>
        ...
    </select>

    <insert>
        ...
    </insert>

    <delete>
        ...
    </delete>

    <update>
        ...
    </update>

</mapper>
```

SqlMapConfig.xml → this file contains database-specific settings, domain object configurations, and mapper files. The structure of the "sqlMapConfig.xml" file is provided below.

```
<?xml version="1.0" encoding="UTF-8" ?>
<!DOCTYPE configuration PUBLIC "-//mybatis.org//DTD Config 3.0//EN"
            "http://mybatis.org/dtd/mybatis-3-config.dtd">

<configuration>

    <!-- MyBatis-specific settings -->
    <settings>
        ...
    </settings>

    <!-- Configure domain objects -->
    <typeAliases>
        ...
    </typeAliases>

    <!-- Configure datasource -->
    <environments default="development">
        <environment id="development">
            <transactionManager type="JDBC"/>
            <dataSource type="POOLED">
                <property name="driver"
                            value="oracle.jdbc.OracleDriver"/>
                <property name="url"
                    value="jdbc:oracle:thin:@localhost:1521:xe"/>
                <property name="username" value="XXXXXX"/>
                <property name="password" value="XXXXXX"/>
            </dataSource>
        </environment>
    </environments>

    <!-- Configure mapper XML files -->
    <mappers>
        ...
```

```
    </mappers>

</configuration>
```

MyBatis with Spring

The following files are used to integrate MyBatis with Spring framework:

1. mapper.xml
2. sqlMapConfig.xml
3. applicationContext.xml

Here, reuse the previously created "mapper.xml" and "sqlMapConfig.xml" files.

ApplicationContext.xml → this file is used to configure the datasource, MyBatis session factory, MyBatis template, and data access objects. The structure of the application context XML file is provided below.

```xml
<?xml version="1.0" encoding="UTF-8"?>
<!DOCTYPE beans PUBLIC "-//SPRING//DTD BEAN//EN"
        "http://www.springframework.org/dtd/spring-beans.dtd">
<beans>

    <!-- Configure datasource -->
    <bean id="dataSource"
        class="org.springframework.jdbc.datasource.
                            DriverManagerDataSource">
        <property name="driverClassName">
            <value>com.mysql.jdbc.Driver</value>
        </property>
        <property name="url">
            <value>jdbc:mysql://localhost:3306/test</value>
        </property>
        <property name="username">
            <value>root</value>
        </property>
        <property name="password">
            <value>mysql</value>
        </property>
    </bean>

    <!-- Configure session factory and load MyBatis configurations -->
    <bean id="sqlSessionFactory"
        class="org.mybatis.spring.SqlSessionFactoryBean">
        <property name="dataSource" ref="dataSource"/>
        <property name="configLocation" value="sqlMapConfig.xml" />
    </bean>

    <!-- Configure MyBatis DB template -->
    <bean id="sqlSessionTemplate"
        class="org.mybatis.spring.SqlSessionTemplate">
        <constructor-arg index="0" ref="sqlSessionFactory"/>
    </bean>
```

```
</beans>
```

The following sections illustrate the complete use of "mapper.xml," "sqlMapConfig.xml," and "applicationContext.xml" files in greater detail. The details of these XML files are discussed later while developing the code examples.

MyBatis (Core)

This section illustrates the Core MyBatis framework for accessing the relational databases. MyBatis provides the `SqlSession` class, which has different methods to execute select, insert, delete, and update statements. The instance of `SqlSession` class is obtained by calling the `openSession()` method of the `SqlSessionFactory` class.

The instance of the `SqlSessionFactory` is obtained by calling the `build()` method of the `SqlSessionFactoryBuilder` class. This build method loads the required MyBatis-specific configurations.

The following utility method can be used to obtain the instance of the `SqlSession` object.

```
public static SqlSession getSqlSession() throws Exception {
    String resource = "core-mybatis-config.xml";
    InputStream inputStream = Resources.getResourceAsStream(resource);
    SqlSessionFactory sqlSessionFactory =
            new SqlSessionFactoryBuilder().build(inputStream);
    return sqlSessionFactory.openSession();
}
```

Example 1: Querying the Data – Select Operations

How to execute SQL statements using MyBatis-provided `SqlSession` class is illustrated in this example. The steps required to implement this example are listed below.

1. Create a data value object (DVO) class.
2. Configure the datasource, data value objects, and MyBatis-specific settings in the XML file.
3. Create a MyBatis-specific "mapper.xml" file.
4. Create a main class to test the code.

The preceding steps are described in the following sections:

Step 1: Create a data value object class

The following data value object is used to map the table data. The "pet" table column values are mapped to the `PetDVO` class attributes.

```
// PetDVO.java
package com.learning.spring.db;

import java.util.Date;
import java.io.Serializable;
```

```
public class PetDVO implements Serializable {

    private Integer id;
    private String name;
    private String owner;
    private String species;
    private String sex;
    private Date birth;
    private Date death;

    // Add getter and setter methods
}
```

Step 2: Configure the datasource, data value objects, and MyBatis-specific settings in the XML file.

This file contains database-specific settings, domain object configurations, and mapper files. The complete XML file is provided below and is named the "core-mybatis-config.xml"

```xml
<?xml version="1.0" encoding="UTF-8" ?>
<!DOCTYPE configuration PUBLIC "-//mybatis.org//DTD Config 3.0//EN"
"http://mybatis.org/dtd/mybatis-3-config.dtd">

<configuration>

    <!-- Configure MyBatis-specifc settings -->
    <settings>
        <setting name="cacheEnabled" value="true"/>
        <setting name="lazyLoadingEnabled" value="true"/>
        <setting name="multipleResultSetsEnabled" value="true"/>
        <setting name="useColumnLabel" value="true"/>
        <setting name="useGeneratedKeys" value="false"/>
        <setting name="defaultExecutorType" value="SIMPLE"/>
        <setting name="defaultStatementTimeout" value="100"/>
    </settings>

    <!-- Configure domain objects -->
    <typeAliases>
        <typeAlias alias="PetDVO"
                type="com.learning.spring.db.mybatis.PetDVO"/>
    </typeAliases>

    <!-- Configure the datasource -->
    <environments default="development">
        <environment id="development">
            <transactionManager type="JDBC"/>
            <dataSource type="POOLED">
                <property name="driver"
                        value="oracle.jdbc.OracleDriver"/>
                <property name="url"
                    value="jdbc:oracle:thin:@localhost:1521:xe"/>
                <property name="username" value="system"/>
                <property name="password" value="PASSWORD"/>
            </dataSource>
        </environment>
    </environments>
```

```
<!-- Configure mapper XML files -->
<mappers>
    <mapper resource="petmapper.xml"/>
</mappers>

</configuration>
```

Step 3: Create a MyBatis-specific "mapper.xml" file.

This file contains database-specific SQL statements such as select, insert, delete, and update. The complete mapper XML file is provided below and is named the "petmapper.xml." This file name is referred in <mappers> section of the "core-mybatis-config.xml" file.

```
<?xml version="1.0" encoding="UTF-8" ?>
<!DOCTYPE mapper PUBLIC "-//mybatis.org//DTD Mapper 3.0//EN"
            "http://mybatis.org/dtd/mybatis-3-mapper.dtd">

<mapper namespace="petmapper">

    <!-- Add SQL statements -->
    <select id="getAllPets" resultType="PetDVO">
        SELECT ID as id, NAME as name, OWNER as owner,
            SPECIES as species,
            SEX as sex, BIRTH as birth, DEATH as death
        FROM Pet
    </select>

</mapper>
```

Let us review the SQL statement.

- select → used for executing the select statements.
- getAllPets → unique name used for identifying the SQL statement.
- resultType → ResultSet return type mapping object.
- NAME, OWNER etc. → represents the database table column names.
- name, owner, etc. (column alias names) → represents domain object properties.

MyBatis maps the database's returned ResultSet to the domain objects. The Java code used to retrieve all pets is provided below.

```
List<PetDVO> petList = getSqlSession().selectList("getAllPets");
```

Step 4: Create a main class to test the code.

Listing 2-1 provides the complete class code; run the following stand-alone class to view the output on console.

Listing 2-1: Stand-alone class to test the MyBatis data access methods

```
// CoreMyBatisMain.java
package com.learning.db.mybatis.core;

import org.apache.ibatis.session.SqlSessionFactory;
```

```java
import org.apache.ibatis.session.SqlSessionFactoryBuilder;
import org.apache.ibatis.session.SqlSession;
import org.apache.ibatis.io.Resources;

import java.io.InputStream;
import java.util.*;

import com.learning.db.mybatis.PetDVO;

public class CoreMyBatisMain {

    public static void main(String[] args) {
        try {
            CoreMyBatisMain main = new CoreMyBatisMain();

            // Printing pets data
            List<PetDVO> allPets = main.getAllPetsData();
            System.out.println("--- allPets ----" + allPets.size());

        } catch (Exception ex) {
            ex.printStackTrace();
        }
    }

    private static SqlSession getSqlSession() throws Exception {
        String resource = "core-mybatis-config.xml";
        InputStream inputStream =
                Resources.getResourceAsStream(resource);
        SqlSessionFactory sqlSessionFactory = new
                SqlSessionFactoryBuilder().build(inputStream);
        return sqlSessionFactory.openSession();
    }

    public List<PetDVO> getAllPetsData() throws Exception {
        return getSqlSession().selectList("getAllPets");
    }
}
```

MyBatis `SqlSession` class provides several methods for executing SQL statements. Let us review each method and its use.

CASE 1: Executing an SQL statement and populating a single domain object.

The following method executes the SQL statement and returns a domain object. Add the following method to the `CoreMyBatisMain` class.

```java
public PetDVO getPetObject(String petName) throws Exception {
    HashMap<String, String> inputMap = new HashMap<String, String>();
    inputMap.put("name", petName);
    return (PetDVO) getSqlSession().selectOne("getPetObject", inputMap);
}
```

The corresponding select statement in the "petmapper.xml" file is provided below. Add the following XML to "petmapper.xml" file.

```xml
<select id="getPetObject" parameterType="java.lang.String"
```

```
        resultType="PetDVO">
      SELECT ID as id, NAME as name, OWNER as owner,SPECIES as species,
          SEX as sex, BIRTH as birth, DEATH as death
      FROM Pet where name = #{name}
</select>
```

Run the `CoreMyBatisMain` class to view the output on the console.

CASE 2: Executing an SQL statement and populating a list of domain objects.

Add the following method to the `CoreMyBatisMain` class. This method executes the SQL statement and maps the ResultSet data into a domain object class.

```
public List<PetDVO> getAllPetsData() throws Exception {
    return getSqlSession().selectList("getAllPets");
}
```

The corresponding select statement in the "petmapper.xml" file is provided below.

```
<select id="getAllPets" resultType="PetDVO">
      SELECT ID as id, NAME as name, OWNER as owner, SPECIES as species,
      SEX as sex, BIRTH as birth, DEATH as death FROM Pet
</select>
```

Run the `CoreMyBatisMain` class to view the output on the console.

CASE 3: Executing an SQL statement and populating a list with column values.

Add the following method to the `CoreMyBatisMain` class. This method executes the SQL statement and maps the ResultSet data into a list.

```
public List<String> getAllSpecies() throws Exception {
    return getSqlSession().selectList("getAllSpecies");
}
```

The corresponding select statement in the "petmapper.xml" file is provided below.

```
<select id="getAllSpecies" resultType="java.lang.String">
    SELECT distinct(SPECIES) as species FROM Pet
</select>
```

Run the `CoreMyBatisMain` class to view the output on the console.

CASE 4: Executing an SQL statement and populating a list based on select criteria.

Add the following method to the `CoreMyBatisMain` class.

```
public List<PetDVO> selectPets(String sex) throws Exception {
    HashMap<String, String> inputMap = new HashMap<String, String>();
    inputMap.put("sex", sex);
    return getSqlSession().selectList("selectPets", inputMap);
}
```

The corresponding select statement in the "petmapper.xml" file is provided below.

In this example, an externally defined parameter map is used to map the return type. The mapping between the column name and bean property name configuration is provided below.

```xml
<resultMap id="petResultMap" type="PetDVO">
    <id property="sex" column="sex"/>
    <result property="id" column="id"/>
    <result property="name" column="name"/>
    <result property="owner" column="owner"/>
    <result property="species" column="species"/>
    <result property="birth" column="birth"/>
    <result property="death" column="death"/>
</resultMap>
```

The "resultMap" attribute of the `<select>` element refers to the externally defined parameter map.

```xml
<select id="selectPets" parameterType="java.lang.String"
                        resultMap="petResultMap">
    SELECT ID as id, NAME as name, OWNER as owner, SPECIES as species,
        SEX as sex, BIRTH as birth, DEATH as death
    FROM Pet where SEX = #{sex}
</select>
```

Run the `CoreMyBatisMain` class to view the output on the console.

The following example illustrates the use of the `SqlSession` class for executing insert statements.

Example 2: Inserting the Data – Insert Operations

Add the following method to the `CoreMyBatisMain` class. This example is used to insert a new record into the "pet" table.

```java
public void createPet(PetDVO petDVO) throws Exception {
    HashMap<String, Object> inputMap = new HashMap<String, Object>();
    inputMap.put("id", petDVO.getId());
    inputMap.put("name", petDVO.getName());
    inputMap.put("owner", petDVO.getOwner());
    inputMap.put("species", petDVO.getSpecies());
    inputMap.put("sex", petDVO.getSex());
    inputMap.put("birth", petDVO.getBirth());

    // Get the sql session and commit the data
    SqlSession sqlSession = getSqlSession();
    sqlSession.insert("createPet", inputMap);
    sqlSession.commit();

    // Printing the generated sequence number (oracle)
    System.out.println("--- Id value ---" + inputMap.get("id"));
}
```

The corresponding insert statement in the "petmapper.xml" file is provided below.

```xml
<insert id="createPet" parameterType="java.util.Map">
    <!-- Generating the next sequence number (oracle) -->
```

```
        <selectKey keyProperty="id" resultType="int" order="BEFORE">
            SELECT PET_ID_SEQ.nextval AS id FROM dual
        </selectKey>

        INSERT INTO Pet (ID, NAME, OWNER, SPECIES, SEX, BIRTH)
        VALUES ( #{id}, #{name}, #{owner}, #{species}, #{sex}, #{birth} )
</insert>
```

Listing 2-2 provides the complete class code; run the following stand-alone class to insert a record into "pet" table.

Listing 2-2: Stand-alone class to insert a record in pet table

```java
// MyBatisMain.java
package com.learning.db.mybatis.core;

import org.apache.ibatis.session.SqlSessionFactory;
import org.apache.ibatis.session.SqlSessionFactoryBuilder;
import org.apache.ibatis.session.SqlSession;
import org.apache.ibatis.io.Resources;
import com.learning.db.mybatis.PetDVO;

public class CoreMyBatisMain {

    public static void main(String[] args) {
        try {
            CoreMyBatisMain main = new CoreMyBatisMain();

            // Setting the data into a domain object
            PetDVO petObj = new PetDVO();
            petObj.setName("Slimmmy");
            petObj.setOwner("Suk");
            petObj.setSpecies("snake");
            petObj.setSex("m");
            petObj.setBirth(new Date());

            // Inserts a record into pet table
            main.createPet(petObj);

        } catch (Exception ex) {
            ex.printStackTrace();
        }
    }
}
```

The following example illustrates the use of the `SqlSession` class for executing update statements.

Example 3: Updating the Data – Update Operations

Add the following method to the `CoreMyBatisMain` class. This example is used to update an existing record in the "pet" table.

```java
public void updatePetData(PetDVO petDVO) throws Exception {
```

```
HashMap<String, Object> inputMap = new HashMap<String, Object>();
inputMap.put("birth", petDVO.getBirth());
inputMap.put("sex", petDVO.getSex());
inputMap.put("name", petDVO.getName());

SqlSession sqlSession = getSqlSession();
sqlSession.update("updatePetData", inputMap);
sqlSession.commit();
}
```

The corresponding update statement in the "petmapper.xml" file is provided below.

```
<update id="updatePetData" parameterType="java.util.Map">
    UPDATE Pet p
    SET p.birth = #{birth}, p.sex = #{sex}
    WHERE p.name = #{name}
</update>
```

Listing 2-3 provides the complete class code; run the following stand-alone class to update a record in "pet" table.

Listing 2-3: Stand-alone class to update a record in pet table

```
// MyBatisMain.java
package com.learning.db.mybatis.core;

import org.apache.ibatis.session.SqlSessionFactory;
import org.apache.ibatis.session.SqlSessionFactoryBuilder;
import org.apache.ibatis.session.SqlSession;
import org.apache.ibatis.io.Resources;
import com.learning.db.mybatis.PetDVO;

public class CoreMyBatisMain {

    public static void main(String[] args) {
        try {
            CoreMyBatisMain main = new CoreMyBatisMain();

            // Setting the data into a domain object
            PetDVO petDataObj = new PetDVO();
            petDataObj.setName("Slimmmy");
            petDataObj.setSex("f");
            petDataObj.setBirth(new Date());

            // Updates the matching record in pet table
            main.updatePetData(petDataObj);

        } catch (Exception ex) {
            ex.printStackTrace();
        }
    }
}
```

The following example illustrates the use of the SqlSession class for executing delete statements.

Example 4: Deleting the Data – Delete Operations

Add the following method to the `CoreMyBatisMain` class. This example is used to delete the matching record from "pet" table.

```
public void deletePet(PetDVO petDVO) throws Exception {
    HashMap<String, String> inputMap = new HashMap<String, String>();
    inputMap.put("species", petDVO.getSpecies());
    inputMap.put("name", petDVO.getName());

    System.out.println("--- deletePet ---" + inputMap);
    SqlSession sqlSession = getSqlSession();
    sqlSession.update("deletePet", inputMap);
    sqlSession.commit();
}
```

The corresponding delete statement in the "petmapper.xml" file is provided below.

```
<delete id="deletePet" parameterType="java.util.Map">
    DELETE FROM Pet
    WHERE name = #{name}
    AND species = #{species}
</delete>
```

Listing 2-4 provides the complete class code; run the following stand-alone class to delete a record from "pet" table.

Listing 2-4: Stand-alone class to delete a matching record

```
// MyBatisMain.java
package com.learning.db.mybatis.core;

import org.apache.ibatis.session.SqlSessionFactory;
import org.apache.ibatis.session.SqlSessionFactoryBuilder;
import org.apache.ibatis.session.SqlSession;
import org.apache.ibatis.io.Resources;
import com.learning.db.mybatis.PetDVO;

public class CoreMyBatisMain {
    public static void main(String[] args) {
        try {
            CoreMyBatisMain main = new CoreMyBatisMain();

            // Setting the data into a domain object
            PetDVO petDataObj = new PetDVO();
            petDataObj.setName("Slimmy1");
            petDataObj.setSpecies("snake");

            // Deletes the matching record
            main.deletePet(petDataObj);
        } catch (Exception ex) {
            ex.printStackTrace();
        }
    }
}
```

MyBatis with Spring

MyBatis can be used with or without Spring integration. This section illustrates the MyBatis integration with Spring framework. Spring provides the `SqlSessionTemplate` class, which uses different methods to execute select, insert, delete, and update statements. This is the utility class used to access the various relational databases. The `SqlSessionTemplate` class encapsulates `SqlSessionFactory`, which is used to establish the database connection.

Spring-based MyBatis Template

`SqlSessionTemplate`: This is the core class used in Spring-based MyBatis for executing SQL statements such as select, insert, delete, and update as well as stored procedures and functions. The `SqlSessionTemplate` class is obtained by injecting the `SqlSessionFactory` reference. An example of a `SqlSessionTemplate` configuration is provided below.

```
<bean id="sqlSessionTemplate"
    class="org.mybatis.spring.SqlSessionTemplate">
    <constructor-arg index="0" ref="sqlSessionFactory"/>
</bean>
```

The datasource reference is injected into the session factory, which includes database-specific details such as server name, database name, user-name, and password. An example session factory configuration is provided below.

```
<bean id="sqlSessionFactory"
    class="org.mybatis.spring.SqlSessionFactoryBean">

    <property name="dataSource" ref="dataSource"/>

    ...
</bean>
```

Example 5: Querying the Data –Select Operations

How to execute SQL statements using the spring-provided `SqlSessionTemplate` class is illustrated in this example. The steps required to implement this example are listed below.

1. Create DAO classes.
2. Create a data value object (DVO) class
3. Configure the datasource and MyBatis-specific classes in an application context file.
4. Create a MyBatis-specific "sqlMapConfig.xml" file.
5. Create a MyBatis-specific "mapper.xml" file.
6. Create a main class to test the code.

The preceding steps are described in the following sections:

Step 1: Create DAO classes.

The `PetDAO` interface has methods used for executing the SQL statements. The complete class code is provided below.

```
// PetDAO.java
package com.learning.spring.db.mybatis;

import java.util.List;

public interface PetDAO {

    List<PetDVO> getAllPetsData();

}
```

The `PetDAOImpl` class implements the above-specified methods. The complete class code is provided below. This class contains methods used for executing select, insert, delete, and update statements.

```
// PetDAOImpl.java
package com.learning.spring.db.mybatis;

import org.mybatis.spring.SqlSessionTemplate;
import java.util.*;

public class PetDAOImpl implements PetDAO {

    private SqlSessionTemplate sqlSessionTemplate;

    public List<PetDVO> getAllPetsData() {
        return (List<PetDVO>)
            sqlSessionTemplate.selectList("getAllPets");
    }

    public void setSqlSessionTemplate(SqlSessionTemplate
                sqlSessionTemplate) {
        this.sqlSessionTemplate = sqlSessionTemplate;
    }
}
```

Step 2: Create a data value object class

The following data value object maps the table data. The "pet" table column values are mapped to the `PetDVO` class attributes.

```
// PetDVO.java
package com.learning.spring.db;

import java.util.Date;
import java.io.Serializable;

public class PetDVO implements Serializable {

    private String name;
    private String owner;
    private String species;
    private String sex;
    private Date birth;
    private Date death;
```

```
        // Add getter and setter methods
}
```

Step 3: Configure the datasource and MyBatis-specific classes in an application context file

The spring application context file is used to configure the datasource, MyBatis session factory, MyBatis template and data access objects. The complete application context XML file is provided below and is named the "applicationContext-myBatis.xml".

```xml
<?xml version="1.0" encoding="UTF-8"?>
<!DOCTYPE beans PUBLIC "-//SPRING//DTD BEAN//EN"
        "http://www.springframework.org/dtd/spring-beans.dtd">
<beans>

    <!-- Configure datasource -->
    <bean id="dataSource"
        class="org.springframework.jdbc.datasource.
                            DriverManagerDataSource">
        <property name="driverClassName">
            <value>com.mysql.jdbc.Driver</value>
        </property>
        <property name="url">
            <value>jdbc:mysql://localhost:3306/test</value>
        </property>
        <property name="username">
            <value>root</value>
        </property>
        <property name="password">
            <value>mysql</value>
        </property>
    </bean>

    <!-- Configure session factory and load myBatis configurations -->
    <bean id="sqlSessionFactory"
        class="org.mybatis.spring.SqlSessionFactoryBean">
        <property name="dataSource" ref="dataSource"/>
        <property name="configLocation" value="sqlMapConfig.xml" />
    </bean>

    <!-- Configure MyBatis DB template -->
    <bean id="sqlSessionTemplate"
        class="org.mybatis.spring.SqlSessionTemplate">
        <constructor-arg index="0" ref="sqlSessionFactory"/>
    </bean>

    <!-- Configure DAO classes -->
    <bean id="petDAOImpl"
        class="com.learning.spring.db.mybatis.PetDAOImpl">
        <property name="sqlSessionTemplate" ref="sqlSessionTemplate"/>
    </bean>

</beans>
```

Step 4: Create a MyBatis-specific "sqlMapConfig.xml" file

This file contains database-specific settings, domain object configurations, and mapper files. The complete XML file is provided below and is named the "sqlMapConfig.xml".

```xml
<?xml version="1.0" encoding="UTF-8" ?>
<!DOCTYPE configuration PUBLIC "-//mybatis.org//DTD Config 3.0//EN"
"http://mybatis.org/dtd/mybatis-3-config.dtd">

<configuration>

    <settings>
        <setting name="cacheEnabled" value="true"/>
        <setting name="lazyLoadingEnabled" value="true"/>
        <setting name="multipleResultSetsEnabled" value="true"/>
        <setting name="useColumnLabel" value="true"/>
        <setting name="useGeneratedKeys" value="false"/>
        <setting name="defaultExecutorType" value="SIMPLE"/>
        <setting name="defaultStatementTimeout" value="100"/>
    </settings>

    <!-- Configure domain objects -->
    <typeAliases>
        <typeAlias alias="PetDVO"
                   type="com.learning.spring.db.mybatis.PetDVO"/>
    </typeAliases>

    <!-- Configure mapper XML files -->
    <mappers>
        <mapper resource="petmapper.xml"/>
    </mappers>

</configuration>
```

Step 5: Create a MyBatis-specific "petmapper.xml" file

This file contains database-specific SQL statements such as select, insert, delete, and update. The complete mapper XML file is provided below and is named the "petmapper.xml"

```xml
<?xml version="1.0" encoding="UTF-8" ?>
<!DOCTYPE mapper PUBLIC "-//mybatis.org//DTD Mapper 3.0//EN"
            "http://mybatis.org/dtd/mybatis-3-mapper.dtd">

<mapper namespace="petmapper">

    <select id="getAllPets" resultType="PetDVO">
        SELECT ID as id, NAME as name, OWNER as owner,
            SPECIES as species,
            SEX as sex, BIRTH as birth, DEATH as death
        FROM Pet
    </select>

</mapper>
```

Let us review the SQL statement.

- select → used for executing the select statements
- getAllPets → unique name used for identifying the SQL statement.

- resultType → ResultSet return type mapping object.
- NAME, OWNER etc. → represents the database table column names.
- name, owner, etc. (column alias names) → represents domain object properties

MyBatis maps the database's returned result set to the application domain objects. The Java code used to retrieve all pets is provided below.

```
List<PetDVO> petList = sqlSessionTemplate.selectList("getAllPets");
```

Step 6: Create a main class to test the code.

Listing 2-5 provides the complete class code; run the following stand-alone class to view the output.

Listing 2-5: Stand-alone class to test the MyBatis DAO methods

```java
// MyBatisMain.java
package com.learning.spring.db.mybatis;

import org.springframework.context.support.
                ClassPathXmlApplicationContext;

import java.util.*;

public class MyBatisMain {

    public static void main(String[] args) {
        try {
            ClassPathXmlApplicationContext appContext =
                new ClassPathXmlApplicationContext(new String[]
                    {"applicationContext-myBatis.xml"});

            PetDAO petDAOImpl = (PetDAO)
                    appContext.getBean("petDAOImpl");

            // Printing pets data
            List<PetDVO> pets = petDAOImpl.getAllPetsData();
            System.out.println("--- pets ---" + pets.size());

        } catch (Exception ex) {
            ex.printStackTrace();
        }
    }
}
```

The MyBatis `SqlSessionTemplate` class provides several methods for executing SQL statements. Let us review each method and its use.

CASE 1: Executing an SQL statement to map a single domain object.

The following method executes an SQL statement and returns a single domain object.

```java
public PetDVO getPetObject(String petName) {
    HashMap<String, String> inputMap = new HashMap<String, String>();
    inputMap.put("name", petName);
```

```
    return (PetDVO)
        sqlSessionTemplate.selectOne("getPetObject", inputMap);
}
```

The corresponding select statement in the "mapper.xml" file is provided below.

```
<select id="getPetObject" parameterType="java.lang.String"
        resultType="PetDVO">
    SELECT ID as id, NAME as name, OWNER as owner,SPECIES as species,
        SEX as sex, BIRTH as birth, DEATH as death
    FROM Pet where name = #{name}
</select>
```

CASE 2: Executing an SQL statement and maps a list of domain objects.

Add the following method to the `PetDAO` interface and its implementation class. This method executes the SQL statement and maps the ResultSet data to a domain object class.

```
public List<PetDVO> getAllPetsData() {
    return (List<PetDVO>) sqlSessionTemplate.selectList("getAllPets");
}
```

The corresponding select statement in the "mapper.xml" file is provided below.

```
<select id="getAllPets" resultType="PetDVO">
    SELECT ID as id, NAME as name, OWNER as owner, SPECIES as species,
        SEX as sex, BIRTH as birth, DEATH as death FROM Pet
</select>
```

CASE 3: Executing an SQL statement and populating a list with column values.

Add the following method to the `PetDAO` interface and its implementation class.

```
public List<String> getAllSpecies() {
    return (List<String>)
            sqlSessionTemplate.selectList("getAllSpecies");
}
```

The corresponding select statement in the "mapper.xml" file is provided below.

```
<select id="getAllSpecies" resultType="java.lang.String">
    SELECT distinct(SPECIES) as species FROM Pet
</select>
```

CASE 4: Executing an SQL statement and populating a list based on select criteria.

Add the following method to the `PetDAO` interface and its implementation class.

```
public List<PetDVO> selectPets(String sex) {
    HashMap<String, String> inputMap = new HashMap<String, String>();
    inputMap.put("sex", sex);
    return (List<PetDVO>)
        sqlSessionTemplate.selectList("selectPets", inputMap);
}
```

The corresponding select statement in the "mapper.xml" file is provided below.

In this example, an externally defined parameter map is used to map the return type. The mapping between the column name and bean property name configuration is provided below.

```xml
<resultMap id="petResultMap" type="PetDVO">
    <id property="sex" column="sex"/>
    <result property="id" column="id"/>
    <result property="name" column="name"/>
    <result property="owner" column="owner"/>
    <result property="species" column="species"/>
    <result property="birth" column="birth"/>
    <result property="death" column="death"/>
</resultMap>
```

The "resultMap" attribute of the `<select>` element refers to the externally defined parameter map.

```xml
<select id="selectPets" parameterType="java.lang.String"
                        resultMap="petResultMap">
    SELECT ID as id, NAME as name, OWNER as owner, SPECIES as species,
        SEX as sex, BIRTH as birth, DEATH as death
    FROM Pet where SEX = #{sex}
</select>
```

The following examples illustrate the use of the `SqlSessionTemplate` class for executing insert statements.

Example 6: Inserting the Data –Insert Operations

Add the following method to the `PetDAO` interface and its implementation class. This example is used to insert a new record in "pet" table.

```java
public void createPet(PetDVO petDVO) {
    HashMap<String, Object> inputMap = new HashMap<String, Object>();
    inputMap.put("name", petDVO.getName());
    inputMap.put("owner", petDVO.getOwner() );
    inputMap.put("species", petDVO.getSpecies() );
    inputMap.put("sex", petDVO.getSex());
    inputMap.put("birth", petDVO.getBirth());
    inputMap.put("death", petDVO.getDeath());

    sqlSessionTemplate.insert("createPet", inputMap);
}
```

The corresponding select statement in the "mapper.xml" file is provided below.

```xml
<insert id="createPet" parameterType="java.util.Map">
    INSERT INTO Pet (NAME, OWNER, SPECIES, SEX, BIRTH, DEATH)
    VALUES (#{name}, #{owner}, #{species}, #{sex}, #{birth}, #{death})
</insert>
```

The following examples illustrate the use of the `SqlSessionTemplate` class for executing update statements.

Example 7: Updating the Data –Update Operations

Add the following method to the `PetDAO` interface and its implementation class. This example is used to update an existing record in the "pet" table.

```
public void updatePetData(PetDVO petDVO) {
    HashMap<String, Object> inputMap = new HashMap<String, Object>();
    inputMap.put("birth", petDVO.getBirth());
    inputMap.put("sex", petDVO.getSex());
    inputMap.put("name", petDVO.getName());

    sqlSessionTemplate.update("updatePetData", inputMap);
}
```

The corresponding select statement in the "mapper.xml" file is provided below.

```
<update id="updatePetData" parameterType="java.util.Map">
    UPDATE Pet p
    SET p.birth = #{birth}, p.sex = #{sex}
    WHERE p.name = #{name}
</update>
```

The following examples illustrate the use of the `SqlSessionTemplate` class for executing delete statements.

Example 8: Deleting the Data –Delete Operations

Add the following method to the `PetDAO` interface and its implementation class. This example is used to delete an existing record in the "pet" table.

```
public void deletePet(PetDVO petDVO) {
    HashMap<String, String> inputMap = new HashMap<String, String>();
    inputMap.put("species", petDVO.getSpecies());
    inputMap.put("name", petDVO.getName());

    sqlSessionTemplate.update("deletePet", inputMap);
}
```

The corresponding select statement in the "mapper.xml" file is provided below.

```
<delete id="deletePet" parameterType="java.util.Map">
    DELETE FROM Pet WHERE name = #{name} AND species = #{species}
</delete>
```


Building and Executing Dynamic SQL Statements

In application development, a common requirement is the building of dynamic SQL statements. MyBatis-provides the most powerful features for building dynamic SQL statements. This section illustrates the building and execution of dynamic SQL statements.

The following statements can be used to build the dynamic SQL statements. The use of the following statements is demonstrated in this section with examples.

- if
- choose-when-otherwise
- foreach
- set

Core MyBatis

This section illustrates the building and execution of dynamic SQL statements using Core MyBatis framework.

CASE 1: Conditionally including the WHERE clause.

Add the following method to the `CoreMyBatisMain` class. This example is used to build the WHERE clause dynamically.

```
public List<PetDVO> findAllSnakes() throws Exception {
    HashMap<String, String> inputMap = new HashMap<String, String>();
    inputMap.put("species", "snake");
    inputMap.put("sex", "f");
    inputMap.put("owner", "De%");

    return getSqlSession().selectList("findAllSnakes", inputMap);
}
```

The corresponding select statement in the "petmapper.xml" file is provided below. The WHERE clause is appended using the `<if>` statement.

```
<select id="findAllSnakes" parameterType="PetDVO" resultType="PetDVO">
    SELECT * FROM Pet WHERE species = #{species}
    <if test="sex != null">
        AND sex = #{sex}
    </if>
    <if test="owner != null">
        AND owner like #{owner}
    </if>
</select>
```

Listing 2-6 provides the complete class code; run the following stand-alone class to view the data from "pet" table.

Listing 2-6: Stand-alone class to view the data

```
// MyBatisMain.java
package com.learning.db.mybatis.core;

import org.apache.ibatis.session.SqlSessionFactory;
import org.apache.ibatis.session.SqlSessionFactoryBuilder;
import org.apache.ibatis.session.SqlSession;
import org.apache.ibatis.io.Resources;
import com.learning.db.mybatis.PetDVO;
```

```
public class CoreMyBatisMain {
    public static void main(String[] args) {
        try {
            CoreMyBatisMain main = new CoreMyBatisMain();
            List<PetDVO> allSnakes = main.findAllSnakes();
            System.out.println("--- all snakes ---" + allSnakes);
        } catch (Exception ex) {
            ex.printStackTrace();
        }
    }
}
```

CASE 2: Building dynamic SQL using the switch statement.

Add the following method to the `CoreMyBatisMain` class. This example is used to build the WHERE clause dynamically.

```
public List<PetDVO> findSnakePets() throws Exception {
    HashMap<String, String> inputMap = new HashMap<String, String>();
    inputMap.put("species", "snake");
    inputMap.put("sex", "f");
    inputMap.put("owner", "De%");
    return getSqlSession().selectList("findSnakePets", inputMap);
}
```

The corresponding select statement in the "petmapper.xml" file is provided below. The WHERE clause is appended using the `<choose>` statement.

```
<select id="findSnakePets" parameterType="PetDVO" resultType="PetDVO">
    SELECT * FROM Pet WHERE species = #{species}
    <choose>
        <when test="sex != null">
            AND sex = #{sex}
        </when>
        <when test="owner != null">
            AND owner like #{owner}
        </when>
        <otherwise>
            AND name like 'Slim%'
        </otherwise>
    </choose>
</select>
```

Run the following stand-alone class to view the data from "pet" table.

```
public class CoreMyBatisMain {
    public static void main(String[] args) {
        try {
            CoreMyBatisMain main = new CoreMyBatisMain();
            List<PetDVO> snakePets = main.findSnakePets();
            System.out.println("--- allSnakes ---" + allSnakes);
        } catch (Exception ex) {
            ex.printStackTrace();
        }
    }
}
```

CASE 3: Building dynamic SQL using the "foreach" statement.

Add the following method to the `CoreMyBatisMain` class. This example is used to build the WHERE clause dynamically.

```
public List<PetDVO> selectPetsIn() throws Exception {
    HashMap<String, Object> inputMap = new HashMap<String, Object>();
    List<String> speciesList = new ArrayList<String>();
    speciesList.add("snake");
    speciesList.add("cat");
    speciesList.add("dog");
    inputMap.put("speciesList", speciesList);
    return getSqlSession().selectList("selectPetsIn",inputMap);
}
```

The corresponding select statement in the "petmapper.xml" file is provided below. The WHERE clause is appended using the `<foreach>` statement.

```
<select id="selectPetsIn" resultType="PetDVO">
    SELECT * FROM Pet P WHERE species IN
    <foreach item="item" index="index" collection="speciesList"
            open="(" separator="," close=")">
        #{item}
    </foreach>
</select>
```

Run the following standalone class to view the data from "pet" table.

```
public class CoreMyBatisMain {
    public static void main(String[] args) {
        try {
            CoreMyBatisMain main = new CoreMyBatisMain();
            List<PetDVO> selectdPets = main.selectPetsIn();
            System.out.println("--- allSnakes ---"+selectdPets);
        } catch (Exception ex) {
            ex.printStackTrace();
        }
    }
}
```

CASE 4: Building an update statement dynamically.

Add the following method to the `CoreMyBatisMain` class. This method dynamically builds the SET clause of an UPDATE statement.

```
public void updatePetDynamically(PetDVO petDVO) throws Exception {
    HashMap<String, Object> inputMap = new HashMap<String, Object>();
    inputMap.put("birth", petDVO.getBirth());
    inputMap.put("death", petDVO.getDeath());
    inputMap.put("sex", petDVO.getSex());
    inputMap.put("name", petDVO.getName());

    System.out.println("--- inputMap ---" + inputMap);
    SqlSession sqlSession = getSqlSession();
    sqlSession.update("updatePetDynamically", inputMap);
```

```
        sqlSession.commit();
}
```

The corresponding update statement in the "petmapper.xml" file is provided below. The UPDATE clause built dynamically using the `<set>` statement.

```
<update id="updatePetDynamically" parameterType="java.util.Map">
    UPDATE Pet
        <set>
            <if test="birth != null">birth=#{birth},</if>
            <if test="death != null">death=#{death},</if>
            <if test="sex != null">sex=#{sex}</if>
        </set>
    WHERE name=#{name}
</update>
```

Run the following stand-alone class to update the data in "pet" table.

```
public class CoreMyBatisMain {
    public static void main(String[] args) {
        try {
            PetDVO petDVO = new PetDVO();
            petDVO.setName("Slim");
            petDVO.setBirth(new Date());
            petDVO.setDeath(new Date());
            petDVO.setSex("m");

            // Updates the data
            main.updatePetDynamically(petDVO);
        } catch (Exception ex) {
            ex.printStackTrace();
        }
    }
}
```

MyBatis with Spring

Similarly, Spring-provided `SqlSessionTemplate` can be used to build and execute the dynamic SQL statements. This section illustrates the building and execution of dynamic SQL statements using MyBatis with Spring.

CASE 1: Conditionally including the WHERE clause.

Add the following method to the `PetDAO` interface and its implementation class. This method builds the SQL statement dynamically and maps the ResultSet data to a domain object class.

```
public List<PetDVO> findAllSnakes() {
    HashMap<String, String> inputMap = new HashMap<String, String>();
    inputMap.put("species", "snake");
    inputMap.put("sex", "f");
    inputMap.put("owner", "Su%");
    return (List<PetDVO>) sqlSessionTemplate.
            selectList("findAllSnakes", inputMap);
}
```

The corresponding select statement in the "petmapper.xml" file is provided below. The WHERE clause is appended using the `<if>` statement.

```
<select id="findAllSnakes" parameterType="PetDVO" resultType="PetDVO">
    SELECT * FROM Pet WHERE species = #{species}
    <if test="sex != null">
        AND sex = #{sex}
    </if>
    <if test="owner != null">
        AND owner like #{owner}
    </if>
</select>
```

CASE 2: Building dynamic SQL using the switch statement.

Add the following method to the `PetDAO` interface and its implementation class. This method builds the WHERE clause dynamically and maps the ResultSet data to a domain object class.

```
public List<PetDVO> findSnakePets() {
    HashMap<String, String> inputMap = new HashMap<String, String>();
    inputMap.put("species", "snake");
    inputMap.put("sex", "f");
    inputMap.put("owner", "Su%");
    return (List<PetDVO>) sqlSessionTemplate.
                selectList("findSnakePets", inputMap);
}
```

The corresponding select statement in the "mapper.xml" file is provided below. The WHERE clause is appended using the `<choose>` statement.

```
<select id="findSnakePets" parameterType="PetDVO" resultType="PetDVO">
    SELECT * FROM Pet WHERE species = #{species}
    <choose>
        <when test="sex != null">
            AND sex = #{sex}
        </when>
        <when test="owner != null">
            AND owner like #{owner}
        </when>
        <otherwise>
            AND name like 'Slim%'
        </otherwise>
    </choose>
</select>
```

CASE 3: Building dynamic SQL using the "foreach" statement.

Add the following method to the `PetDAO` interface and its implementation class. This method builds the WHERE IN select statement dynamically and maps the ResultSet data to a domain object class.

```
public List<PetDVO> selectPetsIn() {
    HashMap<String, Object> inputMap = new HashMap<String, Object>();
    List<String> speciesList = new ArrayList<String>();
    speciesList.add("snake");
```

```
        speciesList.add("cat");
        speciesList.add("dog");
        inputMap.put("speciesList", speciesList);
        return (List<PetDVO>) sqlSessionTemplate.
                selectList("selectPetsIn", inputMap);
}
```

The corresponding select statement in the "mapper.xml" file is provided below. The WHERE IN clause of the select statement is appended using the `<foreach>` statement.

```
<select id="selectPetsIn" resultType="PetDVO">
    SELECT * FROM Pet P WHERE species IN
    <foreach item="item" index="index" collection="speciesList"
            open="(" separator="," close=")">
        #{item}
    </foreach>
</select>
```

CASE 4: Building an update statement dynamically.

Add the following method to the `PetDAO` interface and its implementation class. This method dynamically builds the UPDATE statement.

```
public void updatePetDynamically(PetDVO petDVO) {
    HashMap<String, Object> inputMap = new HashMap<String, Object>();
    inputMap.put("birth", petDVO.getBirth());
    inputMap.put("death", petDVO.getDeath());
    inputMap.put("sex", petDVO.getSex());
    inputMap.put("name", petDVO.getName());

    sqlSessionTemplate.update("updatePetDynamically", inputMap);
}
```

The corresponding update statement in the "petmapper.xml" file is provided below. The UPDATE clause built dynamically using the `<set>` statement.

```
<update id="updatePetDynamically" parameterType="java.util.Map">
    UPDATE Pet
        <set>
            <if test="birth != null">birth=#{birth},</if>
            <if test="death != null">death=#{death},</if>
            <if test="sex != null">sex=#{sex}</if>
        </set>
    WHERE name=#{name}
</update>
```

Association and Nesting Results

How to obtain the nested results using primary and foreign key relationships is illustrated in this section. Figure 1-1 shows the "Employee" and "Dept" tables. The column "DEPTID" of the "EMPLOYEE" table has a foreign key relationship with the column "DEPTID" of the "Dept" table. One department can have multiple employees. How do you obtain the list of employees of a specified department?

Figure 2-1 ER diagram

Figure 2-1 Employee and Department tables

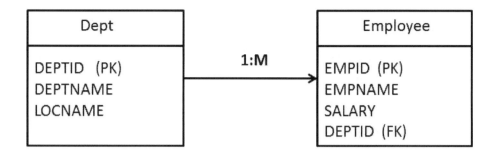

Create the following EMPLOYEE table in your database.

```
CREATE TABLE EMPLOYEE (
     EMPID NUMBER(5,0) NOT NULL,
     EMPNAME VARCHAR2(200),
     SALARY NUMBER(30,0),
     DEPTID NUMBER(5,0) NOT NULL,
     CONSTRAINT EMP_ID_PK PRIMARY KEY (EMPID)
     USING INDEX
)
/
```

Create the following "Dept" table in your database.

```
CREATE TABLE SPOWNER.DEPT (
     DEPTID NUMBER(5,0) NOT NULL,
     DEPTNAME VARCHAR2(200),
     LOCNAME VARCHAR2(200),
     CONSTRAINT DEPT_ID_PK PRIMARY KEY (DEPTID)
     USING INDEX
)
/
```

Add a primary and foreign key relationship between "EMPLOYEE" and "Dept" based on DEPTID column. An example script is provided below.

```
// adding contsraint
ALTER TABLE SPOWNER.EMPLOYEE add constraint FK_EMP_DEPT
FOREIGN KEY (DEPTID) references SPOWNER.DEPT (DEPTID);

// inserting data into DEPT table
INSERT INTO SPOWNER.DEPT VALUES (1, 'IT', 'Arizona');
INSERT INTO SPOWNER.DEPT VALUES (2, 'Servicing', 'IOWA');
INSERT INTO SPOWNER.DEPT VALUES (3, 'Technology', 'TEXAS');

// inserting data into EMPLOYEE table
INSERT INTO SPOWNER.EMPLOYEE VALUES (101, 'John Smith', 10000, 1);
INSERT INTO SPOWNER.EMPLOYEE VALUES (102, 'John Sims', 10000, 1);
INSERT INTO SPOWNER.EMPLOYEE VALUES (103, 'John McCoy', 10000, 2);
```

```
INSERT INTO SPOWNER.EMPLOYEE VALUES (104, 'DeAnne Shaw', 10000, 3);
```

The following example illustrates the above-specified scenario. The steps required to implement this example are listed below.

1. Create data value object (DVO) classes.
2. Configure DVO classes in "core-mybatis-config.xml" file.
3. Define the select statement in "petmapper.xml" file.
4. Create a main class to test the code.

The preceding steps are described in the following sections:

Step 1: Create a data value object (DVO) classes

The following `Employee` and `Dept` classes are used for mapping the ResultSet data. The `Employee` class code is provided below.

```
// Employee.java
package com.learning.db.mybatis;

public class Employee {

    private Integer empId;
    private String empName;
    private Integer salary;

    // Add getter and setter methods
}
```

The `Dept` class code is provided below.

```
// Dept.java
package com.learning.db.mybatis;

import java.util.List;

public class Dept {

    private Integer deptId;
    private String deptName;
    private String locName;
    private List<Employee> employee;

    // Add getter and setter methods
}
```

Step 2: Configure DVO classes in "core-mybatis-config.xml" file.

Configure the domain objects in "core-mybatis-config.xml" file. Here, reuse the previously created "core-mybatis-config.xml" XML file.

```
<typeAliases>
    <typeAlias alias="Employee"
```

```
                    type="com.learning.db.mybatis.Employee"/>
        <typeAlias alias="Dept" type="com.learning.db.mybatis.Dept"/>
</typeAliases>
```

Step 3: Define the select statement in "petmapper.xml" file.

Here, reuse the "petmapper.xml" XML file created in Example-1. Add the following XML elements.

```
<resultMap id="empResult" type="Employee">
    <result property="empId" column="empid"/>
    <result property="empName" column="empname"/>
    <result property="salary" column="salary"/>
</resultMap>

<resultMap id="deptResult" type="Dept">
    <id property="deptId" column="deptid"/>
    <association property="employee" resultMap="empResult"/>
</resultMap>

<select id="getEmployeeAndDeptData" parameterType="java.util.Map"
        resultMap="deptResult">
    SELECT e.empid as empId, e.empname as empName,e.salary as salary
    FROM SPOWNER.Employee e, SPOWNER.dept d
    WHERE e.deptid = d.deptid
    AND d.deptid = #{deptId}
    ORDER BY e.empid
</select>
```

Step 4: Create a main class to test the code.

Listing 2-7 provides the complete class code; run the following stand-alone class to view the output on console.

Listing 2-7: Stand-alone class to test the nested results

```
// CoreMyBatisMain.java
package com.learning.db.mybatis.core;

import org.apache.ibatis.session.SqlSessionFactory;
import org.apache.ibatis.session.SqlSessionFactoryBuilder;
import org.apache.ibatis.session.SqlSession;
import org.apache.ibatis.io.Resources;

import java.io.InputStream;
import java.util.*;

import com.learning.db.mybatis.PetDVO;

public class CoreMyBatisMain {

    public static void main(String[] args) {
        try {
            CoreMyBatisMain main = new CoreMyBatisMain();

            // Printing employee data
```

```java
            Dept dept = main.getEmployeeAndDeptData();
            List<Employee> empList = dept.getEmployee();
            for(Employee employee : empList) {
                System.out.println(employee.getEmpId() +
                    "-" + employee.getEmpName() +
                    "-" + employee.getSalary());
            }

        } catch (Exception ex) {
            ex.printStackTrace();
        }
    }

    private static SqlSession getSqlSession() throws Exception {
        String resource = "core-mybatis-config.xml";
        InputStream inputStream =
                Resources.getResourceAsStream(resource);
        SqlSessionFactory sqlSessionFactory = new
                SqlSessionFactoryBuilder().build(inputStream);
        return sqlSessionFactory.openSession();
    }

    private Dept getEmployeeAndDeptData() throws Exception {
        HashMap<String, Integer> inputMap =
                    new HashMap<String, Integer>();
        inputMap.put("deptId", 1);

        return (Dept) getSqlSession().selectOne
                ("getEmployeeAndDeptData", inputMap);
    }
}
```

Sequence Numbers and Retrieving Auto-Generated Keys

How to use sequence numbers in Oracle, MySQL, and SQL Server databases is illustrated in this section. Oracle database-specific pseudo columns "sequence.nextval" and "sequence.currval" are used to get the next and current value of the sequence number. Other databases such as MySQL and SQL Server, the sequence numbers are auto-generated. These values are often used for primary and unique keys. MyBatis provides a simplified approach to retrieve the auto-generated sequence numbers.

Oracle

The <selectKey> element is used to assign the auto-generated sequence number to the specified keyProperty column. The required XML configuration in "petmapper.xml" file is provided below.

```xml
<insert id="createPet" parameterType="java.util.Map">
    <selectKey keyProperty="id" resultType="int" order="BEFORE">
        SELECT PET_ID_SEQ.nextval AS id FROM dual
    </selectKey>
```

```
      INSERT INTO Pet (ID, NAME, OWNER, SPECIES, SEX, BIRTH)
      VALUES ( #{id}, #{name}, #{owner}, #{species}, #{sex}, #{birth} )
</insert>
```

Refer to the Example -2 for complete details.

MySQL and SQL Server

The useGeneratedKeys=true attribute of the <insert> element is used to assign the auto-generated sequence number to the specified keyProperty column. The required XML configuration in "petmapper.xml" file is provided below.

```
<insert id="insertUser" parameterType="java.util.Map"
        useGeneratedKeys="true" keyProperty="id">
    ...
</insert>
```

How to obtain the value of auto-generated sequence number is illustrated in the following example.

Create the following table in your database.

```
CREATE TABLE USER (
      id MEDIUMINT NOT NULL AUTO_INCREMENT,
      first_name CHAR(30) NULL,
      last_name CHAR(30) NULL,
      PRIMARY KEY (id)
) ENGINE=MyISAM;
```

Use the following User object to map the ResultSet data.

```
public class User {

      private int id;
      private String firstNmae;
      private String lastName;

      // Add getter and setter methods
}
```

Use the following insertUser() method to retrieve the auto-generated key value.

```
public void insertUser() {
    HashMap<String, Object> inputMap = new HashMap<String, Object>();
    User user = new User();
    inputMap.put("id", user.getId());
    inputMap.put("firstName", "John");
    inputMap.put("lastName", "Smith");

    sqlSessionTemplate.insert("insertUser", inputMap);
    System.out.println("--- Id value ---" + inputMap.get("id"));
}
```

The corresponding insert statement in the "mapper.xml" file is provided below. If your database supports auto-generated keys, you can retrieve the generated key value as follows:

```
<insert id="insertUser" parameterType="java.util.Map"
        useGeneratedKeys="true" keyProperty="id">
    INSERT INTO User (first_name, last_name)
    VALUES (#{firstName}, #{lastName})
</insert>
```

Summary

Figure 2-2 summarizes the most important points described in this chapter.

Figure 2-2 Executing SQL statements using MyBatis

This section summarizes the features provided by the MyBatis framework for executing SQL statements.

- MyBatis provided `<select/>`, `<insert/>`, `<delete/>`, and `<update/>` XML tags are used to represent the SQL statements.
- MyBatis provides "if," "foreach," "choose," and "set" statements for building the dynamic SQL statements.
- The primary class used in MyBatis (Core) is `SqlSession`. This class has different methods to execute select, insert, delete, and update statements. The instance of `SqlSession` class is obtained by calling the `openSession()` method of the `SqlSessionFactory` class.
- The `SqlSessionTemplate` class is the core class used in Spring-based MyBatis for executing SQL statements such as select, inserts, delete, and update. This is the MyBatis-Spring utility class used for accessing various relational databases.

- The `<selectKey>` element is used to assign the system generated sequence number to the specified `keyProperty` column. This can be used with databases that support system generated sequence numbers. Example: This can be used while working with the Oracle database.
- The `useGeneratedKeys=true` attribute of the `<insert>` element is used to assign the auto-generated sequence number to the specified `keyProperty` column. This can be used with databases that support auto-generation of primary key values.

Chapter 3. MyBatis Annotations

This chapter illustrates the Annotation-based approach for executing insert, delete, update, and delete statements. MyBatis provides simple and powerful annotations for executing SQL statements. In this approach, it is possible to eliminate the XML configurations completely. MyBatis provided Java API can be used instead of XML-based configurations.

This chapter will discuss the following topics:

- MyBatis annotations
- The various ways of executing select, insert, update, and delete statements using MyBatis annotations
- Working with sequence numbers and retrieval of auto-generated sequence numbers using MyBatis annotations

MyBatis Annotations

MyBatis provides several annotations for executing SQL statements. These annotations are defined in the "org.apache.ibatis.annotations" package. These annotations can be used at field level, method level, class level, and interface level, as well as with method parameters. The following section explains the commonly used annotations for executing SQL statements. Each annotation is demonstrated with a code example.

- @Select
- @Insert
- @Delete
- @Update
- @Options
- @SelectKey
- @Param
- @Results
- @Result

@Select

This annotation represents the SQL select statement. This annotation is used at the method level. This annotation is equivalent to the `<select/>` element in an XML-based configuration. An example of the use of an `@Select` annotation is given below.

```
@Select(" SELECT ID as id, NAME as name, OWNER as owner, SPECIES as " +
        " species, SEX as sex, BIRTH as birth, DEATH as death " +
        " FROM Pet where name = #{name} ")
public PetDVO getPetObject(String petName);
```

The equivalent XML configuration in "petmapper.xml" file is provided below.

```
<select id="getPetObject" parameterType="java.lang.String"
```

```
                    resultType="PetDVO">
    SELECT ID as id, NAME as name, OWNER as owner,
        SPECIES as species, SEX as sex,
        BIRTH as birth, DEATH as death
    FROM Pet where name = #{name}
</select>
```

@Insert

This annotation represents the SQL insert statement. This annotation is used at the method level. This annotation is equivalent to the `<insert/>` element in an XML-based configuration. An example of the use of an `@Insert` annotation is given below.

```
@Insert("INSERT INTO Pet (ID, NAME, OWNER, SPECIES, SEX, BIRTH) " +
    " VALUES (#{id}, #{name}, #{owner}, #{species}, #{sex}, #{birth})")
public void insertPetData(PetDVO petDVO);
```

The equivalent XML configuration in "petmapper.xml" file is provided below.

```
<insert id="insertPetData" parameterType="java.util.Map">
    INSERT INTO Pet (ID, NAME, OWNER, SPECIES, SEX, BIRTH)
    VALUES (#{id}, #{name}, #{owner}, #{species}, #{sex}, #{birth})
</insert>
```

@Delete

This annotation represents the SQL delete statement. This annotation is used at the method level. This annotation is equivalent to the `<delete/>` element in an XML-based configuration. An example of the use of an `@Delete` annotation is given below.

```
@Delete("DELETE FROM Pet WHERE name = #{name} AND species = #{species}")
public void deletePet(PetDVO petDVO);
```

The equivalent XML configuration in "petmapper.xml" file is provided below.

```
<delete id="deletePet" parameterType="java.util.Map">
    DELETE FROM Pet WHERE name = #{name} AND species = #{species}
</delete>
```

@Update

This annotation represents the SQL update statement. This annotation is used at the method level. This annotation is equivalent to the `<update/>` element in an XML-based configuration. An example of the use of an `@Update` annotation is given below.

```
@Update(" UPDATE Pet p SET p.birth = #{birth}, p.sex = #{sex} " +
        " WHERE p.name = #{name} ")
public void updatePetData(PetDVO petDVO);
```

The equivalent XML configuration in "petmapper.xml" file is provided below.

```
<update id="updatePetData" parameterType="java.util.Map">
    UPDATE Pet p SET p.birth = #{birth}, p.sex = #{sex}
    WHERE p.name = #{name}
</update>
```

@SelectKey

This annotation represents the primary and unique key columns of a table. This annotation is used at the method level. This annotation is used with @Insert-annotated methods. This annotation is equivalent to the <selectKey/> element in an XML-based configuration. An example of the use of an @SelectKey annotation is given below.

```
@Insert(" INSERT INTO Pet (ID, NAME, OWNER, SPECIES, SEX, BIRTH) " +
    " VALUES (#{id}, #{name}, #{owner}, #{species}, #{sex}, #{birth})")
@SelectKey(statement="SELECT PET_ID_SEQ.nextval AS id FROM dual",
        keyProperty="id",
        before=true,
        resultType=int.class)
public void insertPet(PetDVO petDVO);
```

The equivalent XML configuration in "petmapper.xml" file is provided below.

```
<insert id="insertPet" parameterType="java.util.Map">
    <selectKey keyProperty="id" resultType="int" order="BEFORE">
        SELECT PET_ID_SEQ.nextval AS id FROM dual
    </selectKey>

    INSERT INTO Pet (ID, NAME, OWNER, SPECIES, SEX, BIRTH)
    VALUES (#{id}, #{name}, #{owner}, #{species}, #{sex}, #{birth})
</insert>
```

@Param

This annotation represents method parameters. This annotation is used with method parameters. This annotation is equivalent to the #{param} in an XML-based configuration. An example of the use of an @Param annotation is given below. The method parameter @Param("birth") maps to the #{birth} defined in the update statement.

```
@Update(" UPDATE Pet SET birth = #{birth}, sex = #{sex} " +
        " WHERE name = #{name} ")
public void updateData(@Param("birth") Date birth,
                       @Param("sex") String sex,
                       @Param("name") String name);
```

The equivalent XML configuration in "petmapper.xml" file is provided below.

```
<update id="updatePetData" parameterType="java.util.Map">
    UPDATE Pet p SET p.birth = #{birth}, p.sex = #{sex}
    WHERE p.name = #{name}
</update>
```

@Result

This annotation represents the mapping between database column and object property. This annotation is used at the method level. This annotation is equivalent to the `<result>` and `<id>` in an XML-based configuration. An example of the use of an `@Result` annotation is given below.

```
@Results(value = {
    @Result(property = "id", column = "ID"),
    @Result(property = "name", column = "NAME"),
    @Result(property = "owner", column = "OWNER"),
    @Result(property = "species", column = "SPECIES"),
    @Result(property = "sex", column = "SEX")
})
```

The equivalent XML configuration in "petmapper.xml" file is provided below.

```
<resultMap id="petResultMap" type="PetDVO">
    <id property="sex" column="sex"/>
    <result property="id" column="id"/>
    <result property="name" column="name"/>
    <result property="owner" column="owner"/>
    <result property="species" column="species"/>
    <result property="birth" column="birth"/>
    <result property="death" column="death"/>
</resultMap>
```

@Results

This annotation represents a list of return values. This annotation is used at the method level. This annotation is equivalent to the `<resultMap>` in an XML-based configuration. An example of the use of an `@Results` annotation is given below.

```
@Select("SELECT * FROM PET")
@Results(value = {
    @Result(property = "id", column = "ID"),
    @Result(property = "name", column = "NAME"),
    @Result(property = "owner", column = "OWNER"),
    @Result(property = "species", column = "SPECIES"),
    @Result(property = "sex", column = "SEX")
})
List<PetDVO> selectAllPets();
```

The equivalent XML configuration in "petmapper.xml" file is provided below.

```
<resultMap id="petResultMap" type="PetDVO">
    <id property="sex" column="sex"/>
    <result property="id" column="id"/>
    <result property="name" column="name"/>
    <result property="owner" column="owner"/>
    <result property="species" column="species"/>
    <result property="birth" column="birth"/>
    <result property="death" column="death"/>
</resultMap>
```

```
<select id="selectPets" parameterType="java.lang.String"
            resultMap="petResultMap">
    SELECT ID as id, NAME as name, OWNER as owner,
        SPECIES as species, SEX as sex,
        BIRTH as birth, DEATH as death
    FROM Pet where sex = #{sex}
</select>
```

@Options

This annotation is used to specify the attributes of mapped statements. This annotation is used at the method level. This annotation is equivalent to the element attributes specified in an XML-based configuration. An example of the use of an @Options annotation is given below.

```
@Insert("INSERT INTO User (first_name, last_name) " +
    " VALUES (#{firstName}, #{lastName} ")
@Options(useGeneratedKeys = true, keyProperty = "id")
public void insertUser(User user);
```

The equivalent XML configuration in "mapper.xml" file is provided below.

```
<insert id="insertUser" parameterType="java.util.Map"
        useGeneratedKeys="true" keyProperty="id">
    INSERT INTO User (first_name, last_name)
    VALUES (#{firstName}, #{lastName})
</insert>
```

Demo Examples

Example 1: Select-Insert-Delete-Update Operations Using Annotations

How to execute SQL statements using the MyBatis-provided SqlSession class is illustrated in this example. The steps required to implement this example are listed below.

1. Create a data value object (DVO) class.
2. Configure the data source, data value objects, and MyBatis-specific settings in XML file.
3. Create a mapper interface.
4. Create a DAO class.
5. Create a main class to test the code.

The preceding steps are described in the following sections:

Step 1: Create a data value object class

The following data value object maps the table data. The "pet" table column values are mapped to the PetDVO class attributes.

```
// PetDVO.java
package com.learning.spring.db;
```

```
import java.util.Date;
import java.io.Serializable;

public class PetDVO implements Serializable {

    private Integer id;
    private String name;
    private String owner;
    private String species;
    private String sex;
    private Date birth;
    private Date death;

    // Add getter and setter methods
}
```

Step 2: Configure the datasource and MyBatis-specific settings in XML file.

This file contains database and MyBatis-specific settings. The complete XML file is provided below and is named the "java-mybatis-config.xml". It is possible to eliminate this file completely, if you decided to use Java API. In this example, MyBatis Java API is used to configure the mapper configurations.

```xml
<?xml version="1.0" encoding="UTF-8" ?>
<!DOCTYPE configuration PUBLIC "-//mybatis.org//DTD Config 3.0//EN"
"http://mybatis.org/dtd/mybatis-3-config.dtd">

<configuration>

    <!-- Configure MyBatis-specifc settings -->
    <settings>
        <setting name="cacheEnabled" value="true"/>
        <setting name="lazyLoadingEnabled" value="true"/>
        <setting name="multipleResultSetsEnabled" value="true"/>
        <setting name="useColumnLabel" value="true"/>
        <setting name="useGeneratedKeys" value="false"/>
        <setting name="defaultExecutorType" value="SIMPLE"/>
        <setting name="defaultStatementTimeout" value="100"/>
    </settings>

    <!-- Configure the data source -->
    <environments default="development">
        <environment id="development">
            <transactionManager type="JDBC"/>
            <dataSource type="POOLED">
                <property name="driver"
                          value="oracle.jdbc.OracleDriver"/>
                <property name="url"
                    value="jdbc:oracle:thin:@localhost:1521:xe"/>
                <property name="username" value="system"/>
                <property name="password" value="PASSWORD"/>
            </dataSource>
        </environment>
    </environments>
</configuration>
```

Step 3: Create a mapper interface.

In case of an annotation-based approach, the mapper XML configurations are replaced with Java interface. This interface has all the methods with required annotations. The following `PetMapper` interface is equivalent to the "petmapper.xml" file created in XML-based implementation.

```java
// PetMapper.java
package com.learning.db.mybatis.java;

import org.apache.ibatis.annotations.*;
import com.learning.db.mybatis.PetDVO;
import java.util.*;

public interface PetMapper {

    // Selecting a single pet
    @Select("SELECT ID as id, NAME as name, OWNER as owner,SPECIES as" +
                " species, SEX as sex, " +
                " BIRTH as birth, DEATH as death " +
                " FROM Pet where name = #{name} ")
    public PetDVO getPetObject(String petName);

    // Selecting all pets
    @Select("SELECT * FROM PET")
    @Results(value = {
        @Result(property = "id", column = "ID"),
        @Result(property = "name", column = "NAME"),
        @Result(property = "owner", column = "OWNER"),
        @Result(property = "species", column = "SPECIES"),
        @Result(property = "sex", column = "SEX")
    })
    List<PetDVO> selectAllPets();

    // Selecting all pets
    @Select(" SELECT ID as id, NAME as name, OWNER as owner, SPECIES as+
        " species,SEX as sex, BIRTH as birth, DEATH as death FROM Pet")
    public List<PetDVO> getAllPetsData();

    // Select all matching pets based on a criteria
    @Select(" SELECT ID as id, NAME as name, OWNER as owner, SPECIES as+
        " species, SEX as sex, BIRTH as birth, DEATH as death" +
        " FROM Pet where sex = #{sex} ")
    public List<PetDVO> selectPets(String sex);

    // Updating pet data
    @Update("UPDATE Pet p SET p.birth = #{birth}, p.sex = #{sex} WHERE "
        + " p.name = #{name} ")
    public void updatePetData(PetDVO petDVO);

    // Updating pet data
    @Update(" UPDATE Pet SET birth = #{birth}, sex = #{sex} " +
            " WHERE name = #{name} ")
    public void updateData(@Param("birth") Date birth,
                           @Param("sex") String sex,
                           @Param("name") String name);

    // Deleting pet data
```

```
@Delete(" DELETE FROM Pet WHERE name = #{name} " +
        " AND species = #{species} ")
public void deletePet(PetDVO petDVO);

// Inserting a new record
@Insert(" INSERT INTO Pet (ID, NAME, OWNER, SPECIES, SEX, BIRTH) " +
        " VALUES (#{id}, #{name}, #{owner}, #{species}, #{sex}, " +
        " #{birth}) ")
@SelectKey(statement="SELECT PET_ID_SEQ.nextval AS id FROM dual",
        keyProperty="id",
        before=true,
        resultType=int.class)
public void insertPet(PetDVO petDVO);

}
```

Step 4: Create a DAO class.

The following `PetDAOImpl` class implements the above specified interface methods. The complete class code is provided below. This class contains methods used for executing select, insert, delete, and update statements.

```
// PetDAOImpl.java
package com.learning.db.mybatis.java;

import org.apache.ibatis.session.SqlSession;
import org.apache.ibatis.session.SqlSessionFactory;
import org.apache.ibatis.session.SqlSessionFactoryBuilder;
import org.apache.ibatis.io.Resources;

import java.io.InputStream;
import java.util.*;

import com.learning.db.mybatis.PetDVO;

public class PetDAOImpl {

    // Loads the configuration settings, creates a sql session.
    private static SqlSession getSqlSession() throws Exception {
        String resource = "java-mybatis-config.xml";
        InputStream inputStream =
            Resources.getResourceAsStream(resource);
        SqlSessionFactory sqlSessionFactory =
                new SqlSessionFactoryBuilder().build(inputStream);
        sqlSessionFactory.getConfiguration().
                addMapper(PetMapper.class);

        return sqlSessionFactory.openSession();
    }

    public List<PetDVO> getAllPetsData() throws Exception {
        PetMapper mapper = getSqlSession().getMapper(PetMapper.class);
        return mapper.getAllPetsData();
    }

    public PetDVO getPetObject(String petName) throws Exception {
```

```java
        PetMapper mapper = getSqlSession().getMapper(PetMapper.class);
        return mapper.getPetObject(petName);
    }

    List<PetDVO> selectAllPets() throws Exception {
        PetMapper mapper = getSqlSession().getMapper(PetMapper.class);
        return mapper.selectAllPets();
    }

    public List<PetDVO> selectPets(String sex) throws Exception {
        PetMapper mapper = getSqlSession().getMapper(PetMapper.class);
        return mapper.selectPets(sex);
    }

    public void updatePetData(PetDVO petDVO) throws Exception {
        SqlSession sqlSession = getSqlSession();
        PetMapper mapper = sqlSession.getMapper(PetMapper.class);
        mapper.updatePetData(petDVO);

        sqlSession.commit();
    }

    public void updateData(Date birth, String sex, String name)
            throws Exception {
        SqlSession sqlSession = getSqlSession();
        PetMapper mapper = sqlSession.getMapper(PetMapper.class);
        mapper.updateData(birth, sex, name);

        sqlSession.commit();
    }

    public void deletePet(PetDVO petDVO) throws Exception {
        SqlSession sqlSession = getSqlSession();
        PetMapper mapper = sqlSession.getMapper(PetMapper.class);

        mapper.deletePet(petDVO);
        sqlSession.commit();
    }

    public void insertPet(PetDVO petDVO) throws Exception {
        SqlSession sqlSession = getSqlSession();
        PetMapper mapper = sqlSession.getMapper(PetMapper.class);
        mapper.insertPet(petDVO);
        sqlSession.commit();

        // Printing the generated key value
        System.out.println("--- Id value ---" + petDVO.getId());
    }
}
```

Step 5: Create a main class to test the code.

Listing 3-1 provides the complete class code; run the following stand-alone class to view the output on console.

Listing 3-1: Stand-alone class to test the annotated interface methods

```java
// JavaMyBatisMain.java
package com.learning.db.mybatis.java;

import java.util.*;
import com.learning.db.mybatis.PetDVO;

public class JavaMyBatisMain {

    public static void main(String[] args) {
        try {
            JavaMyBatisMain main = new JavaMyBatisMain();

            // Calling the private methods
            main.selectAllPets();

        } catch (Exception ex) {
            ex.printStackTrace();
        }
    }

    private void getPetObject() throws Exception {
        PetDAOImpl petDAOImpl = new PetDAOImpl();
        PetDVO pet = petDAOImpl.getPetObject("Fluffy");
        System.out.println("----- pet ------" + pet);
    }

    private void getAllPetsData() throws Exception {
        PetDAOImpl petDAOImpl = new PetDAOImpl();
        List<PetDVO> allPets = petDAOImpl.getAllPetsData();
        System.out.println("----- size ------" + allPets.size());
    }

    private void selectPets() throws Exception {
        PetDAOImpl petDAOImpl = new PetDAOImpl();
        List<PetDVO> allPetsData = petDAOImpl.selectPets("f");
        System.out.println("----- size ------" + allPetsData.size());
    }

    private void selectAllPets() throws Exception {
        PetDAOImpl petDAOImpl = new PetDAOImpl();
        List<PetDVO> allPetsData = petDAOImpl.selectAllPets();
        System.out.println("----- size ------" + allPetsData.size());
    }

    private void updatePetData() throws Exception {
        PetDAOImpl petDAOImpl = new PetDAOImpl();
        PetDVO petDataObj = new PetDVO();
        petDataObj.setName("Slimmmy");
        petDataObj.setSex("m");
        petDataObj.setBirth(new Date());
        petDAOImpl.updatePetData(petDataObj);
    }

    private void updateData() throws Exception {
        PetDAOImpl petDAOImpl = new PetDAOImpl();
```

```
            PetDVO petDataObj = new PetDVO();
            petDataObj.setName("Slimmmy");
            petDataObj.setSex("m");
            petDataObj.setBirth(new Date());
            petDAOImpl.updateData(new Date(), "m", "Slim");
        }

    private void deletePet() throws Exception {
            PetDAOImpl petDAOImpl = new PetDAOImpl();
            PetDVO petDVO = new PetDVO();
            petDVO.setName("Slimmmy1");
            petDVO.setSpecies("snake");
            petDAOImpl.deletePet(petDVO);
        }

    private void insertPet() throws Exception {
            PetDAOImpl petDAOImpl = new PetDAOImpl();
            PetDVO petObj = new PetDVO();
            petObj.setName("Slimmy");
            petObj.setOwner("Danny");
            petObj.setSpecies("snake");
            petObj.setSex("f");
            petObj.setBirth(new Date());

            petDAOImpl.insertPet(petObj);
        }
    }
```

Summary

This section summarizes the features provided by the MyBatis framework for executing SQL statements.

- MyBatis provided @Select, @Insert, @Delete, and @Update annotations represent the SQL select, insert, delete, and update statements.
- The primary class used in MyBatis (Core) is SqlSession. This class has different methods to execute select, insert, delete, and update statements. The instance of SqlSession class is obtained by calling the openSession() method of the SqlSessionFactory class. The getConfiguration().addMapper(...) method of SqlSessionFactory class is used to add a mapper class.
- The @SelectKey annotation is used to assign the system generated sequence number to the specified keyProperty column. This can be used with databases that support system generated sequence numbers.
- The @Options annotation is used to specify the attributes of mapped statements. This annotation is equivalent to the <insert/> element attributes specified in XML-based configuration.

Figure 3-1 summarizes the most important points described in this chapter.

Figure 3-1 Executing SQL statements using MyBatis-provided annotations

Chapter 4. Executing Stored Procedures and Functions

The most common requirement while working with enterprise application development is the support for database stored procedures and functions. Application developers quite often deal with stored procedures and functions for implementing the business functionality. MyBatis framework provides a simplified approach for executing stored procedures and functions. MyBatis supports both XML and Annotation-based approaches for executing stored procedures and functions. This chapter illustrates the XML and Annotation-based approaches for executing database stored procedures and functions using the MyBatis framework.

This chapter will discuss the following topics:

- MyBatis support for executing stored procedures and functions
- XML-based approach for executing stored procedures and functions
- Annotation-based approach for executing stored procedures and functions
- How to use IN, OUT, and CURSOR data type parameters while executing the stored procedures

Prerequisite and Setting -Up the Environment

This section illustrates the configurations required for executing the stored procedures and functions.

- Make sure "read_all_pets" and "callReadPet" stored procedures are created in your database.
- Make sure "callPetOwnerFunction" is created in your database.
- Chapter -1 provides the complete details of the above-specified stored procedures and functions.

Executing Stored Procedures and Functions (XML-based)

This section illustrates the XML-based approach for executing stored procedures and functions.

Example 1: How to Execute Stored Procedures –IN and OUT Parameters

How to execute database stored procedures using Spring-provided `SqlSessionTemplate` class is illustrated in this example. The definition of the stored procedure is provided below.

```
CREATE OR REPLACE PROCEDURE read_pet(
    in_name IN VARCHAR2,
    out_owner OUT VARCHAR2,
    out_species OUT VARCHAR2,
    out_sex OUT VARCHAR2,
    out_birth OUT DATE,
    out_death OUT DATE
)
```

This "read_pet(...)" stored procedure has one IN parameter and five OUT parameters. This procedure returns the data in OUT parameters for a given input.

The steps required to implement this example are listed below.

1. Create a data value object (DVO) class.
2. Create a MyBatis-specific "sqlMapConfig.xml" file.
3. Configure the datasource and MyBatis-specific classes in the Spring application context file.
4. Create a MyBatis-specific "petmapper.xml" file.
5. Create a DAO class and its implementation.
6. Create a main class to test the code.

The preceding steps are described in the following sections:

Step 1: Create a data value object class

The following data value object maps the table data. The "pet" table column values are mapped to the PetDVO class attributes.

```
// PetDVO.java
package com.learning.spring.db;

import java.util.Date;
import java.io.Serializable;

public class PetDVO implements Serializable {

    private Integer id;
    private String name;
    private String owner;
    private String species;
    private String sex;
    private Date birth;
    private Date death;

    // Add getter and setter methods
}
```

Step 2: Create a MyBatis-specific "sqlMapConfig.xml" file.

Here, reuse the previously created "sqlMapConfig.xml" file. Refer to Chapter -2 for complete details.

Step 3: Configure the datasource and MyBatis-specific classes in the Spring application context file.

Here, reuse the previously created "applicationContext-myBatis.xml" file. Refer to Chapter -2 for complete details.

Step 4: Create a MyBatis-specific "petmapper.xml" file.

This file contains database-specific SQL statements for executing stored procedures. The complete mapper XML file is provided below and is named the "petmapper.xml."

```
<?xml version="1.0" encoding="UTF-8" ?>
```

Executing Stored Procedures and Functions (XML-based)

```
<!DOCTYPE mapper PUBLIC "-//mybatis.org//DTD Mapper 3.0//EN"
            "http://mybatis.org/dtd/mybatis-3-mapper.dtd">

<mapper namespace="petmapper">

    <select id="callReadPet" parameterType="java.util.Map"
            resultType="java.util.Map" statementType="CALLABLE">
        { CALL read_pet(
            #{name, mode=IN, jdbcType=VARCHAR},
            #{owner, mode=OUT, jdbcType=VARCHAR},
            #{species, mode=OUT, jdbcType=VARCHAR},
            #{sex, mode=OUT, jdbcType=VARCHAR},
            #{birth, mode=OUT, jdbcType=DATE},
            #{death, mode=OUT, jdbcType=DATE}
        )}
    </select>

</mapper>
```

Step 5: Create a DAO class and its implementation.

The `PetDAO` interface contains methods used for executing stored procedures. The complete interface definition is provided below.

```
// PetDAO.java
package com.learning.spring.db.mybatis;

import java.util.List;

public interface PetDAO {

    void callReadPet();
}
```

The `PetDAOImpl` class implements the above specified methods. The complete class code is provided below.

```
// PetDAOImpl.java
package com.learning.spring.db.mybatis;

import org.mybatis.spring.SqlSessionTemplate;
import java.util.*;

public class PetDAOImpl implements PetDAO {

    private SqlSessionTemplate sqlSessionTemplate;

    public void callReadPet() {
        HashMap<String,String> inputMap = new HashMap<String,String>();
        inputMap.put("name", "Slimmy");
        inputMap.put("owner", "");
        inputMap.put("species", "");
        inputMap.put("sex", "");
        inputMap.put("birth", "");
        inputMap.put("death", "");
```

```
        sqlSessionTemplate.selectOne("callReadPet", inputMap);

        // Prints the procedure output data
        System.out.println("--- owner ---" + inputMap.get("owner"));
        System.out.println("--- species --" + inputMap.get("species"));
        System.out.println("--- sex ---" + inputMap.get("sex"));
    }
}
```

Step 6: Create a main class to test the code.

Listing 4-1 provides the complete class code; run the following stand-alone class to view the output on console.

Listing 4-1: Stand-alone class to test the stored procedure

```
// MyBatisTestStoredProcedures.java
package com.learning.db.mybatis;

import org.springframework.context.support.
                ClassPathXmlApplicationContext;
import java.util.List;

public class MyBatisTestStoredProcedures {

    public static void main(String[] args) {
        try {
            ClassPathXmlApplicationContext appContext =
                new ClassPathXmlApplicationContext(new String[]
                    {"applicationContext-myBatis.xml"});

            PetDAO petDAOImpl = (PetDAO)
                        appContext.getBean("petDAOImpl");
            petDAOImpl.callReadPet();

        } catch (Exception ex) {
            ex.printStackTrace();
        }
    }
}
```

Example 2: How to Execute Stored Procedures – CURSOR Parameters

How to execute a stored procedure that returns the result set data as a database cursor is illustrated in this example. The definition of the executed stored procedure is provided below.

```
CREATE OR REPLACE PROCEDURE read_all_pets(c_allpets OUT SYS_REFCURSOR)
```

This "read_all_pets(...)" stored procedure returns the result set data as a database CURSOR.

The steps required to implement this example are listed below.

1. Create a data value object (DVO) class.
2. Create a MyBatis-specific "sqlMapConfig.xml" file.

3. Configure the datasource and MyBatis-specific classes in the Spring application context file.
4. Create a MyBatis-specific "petmapper.xml" file.
5. Create a DAO class and its implementation.
6. Create a main class to test the code.

The preceding steps are described in the following sections:

Step 1, Step 2 and Step 3:

Here, follow the steps specified in Example -1

Step 4: Create a MyBatis-specific "petmapper.xml" file.

Here, reuse the "petmapper.xml" file created in Example-1. Add the following XML to the "petmapper.xml" file. The following syntax is recommended for Oracle-based stored procedures.

```
<resultMap id="cursorData" type="PetDVO">
    <result property="sex" column="sex"/>
    <result property="name" column="name"/>
    <result property="owner" column="owner"/>
    <result property="species" column="species"/>
    <result property="birth" column="birth"/>
    <result property="death" column="death"/>
</resultMap>

<select id="callReadAllPets" parameterType="java.util.Map"
                        statementType="CALLABLE">
    { CALL read_all_pets( #{petData, mode=OUT, jdbcType=CURSOR,
        javaType=ResultSet, resultMap=cursorData} ) }
</select>
```

NOTE: The following `<select>` statement syntax is valid for MySQL-based stored procedure. The following syntax is recommended for MySQL-based stored procedures.

```
<select id="callReadAllPets" resultType="PetDVO"
        statementType="CALLABLE">
    { CALL read_all_pets() }
</select>
```

Step 5: Create a DAO class and its implementation.

The `PetDAO` interface contains methods used for executing stored procedures. The complete interface definition is provided below.

```
// PetDAO.java
package com.learning.spring.db.mybatis;

import java.util.List;

public interface PetDAO {

    List<PetDVO> callReadAllPets();
}
```

The `PetDAOImpl` class implements the above specified methods. The complete class code is provided below.

```java
// PetDAOImpl.java
package com.learning.spring.db.mybatis;

import org.mybatis.spring.SqlSessionTemplate;
import java.util.*;

public class PetDAOImpl implements PetDAO {

    private SqlSessionTemplate sqlSessionTemplate;

    public List<PetDVO> callReadAllPets() {
        HashMap<String, List<PetDVO>> inputMap =
                        new HashMap<String, List<PetDVO>>();
        List<PetDVO> petList = new ArrayList<PetDVO>();
        inputMap.put("petData", petList);

        sqlSessionTemplate.selectList("callReadAllPets", inputMap);
        List<PetDVO> outputData = inputMap.get("petData");
        return outputData;
    }
}
```

Step 6: Create a main class to test the code.

Listing 4-2 provides the complete class code; run the following stand-alone class to view the output on console.

Listing 4-2: Stand-alone class to test the stored procedure

```java
// MyBatisTestStoredProcedures.java
package com.learning.db.mybatis;

import org.springframework.context.support.
                    ClassPathXmlApplicationContext;
import java.util.List;

public class MyBatisTestStoredProcedures {

    public static void main(String[] args) {
        try {
            ClassPathXmlApplicationContext appContext =
                new ClassPathXmlApplicationContext(new String[]
                    {"applicationContext-myBatis.xml"});

            PetDAO petDAOImpl = (PetDAO)
                        appContext.getBean("petDAOImpl");

            List<PetDVO> procResult = petDAOImpl.callReadAllPets();

            // Prints the output on console
            System.out.println("---procResult---" + procResult.size());
            for (PetDVO petDVObj : procResult) {
                System.out.println("---name---" + petDVObj.getName());
            }
```

```
        } catch (Exception ex) {
            ex.printStackTrace();
        }
    }
}
```

Example 3: How to Execute Stored Functions

How to execute database stored functions using Spring-provided `SqlSessionTemplate` class is illustrated in this example. The definition of the stored function is provided below.

```
CREATE OR REPLACE FUNCTION get_pet_owner(in_petname IN VARCHAR2) RETURN
VARCHAR2 IS out_owner VARCHAR2(200);
```

This "get_pet_owner(...)" stored function returns the owner name for the given input.

The steps required to implement this example are listed below.

1. Create a data value object (DVO) class.
2. Create a MyBatis-specific "sqlMapConfig.xml" file.
3. Configure the datasource and MyBatis-specific classes in the Spring application context file.
4. Create a MyBatis-specific "petmapper.xml" file.
5. Create a DAO class and its implementation.
6. Create a main class to test the code.

The preceding steps are described in the following sections:

Step 1, Step 2 and Step 3:

Here, follow the steps specified in Example-1

Step 4: Create a MyBatis-specific "petmapper.xml" file.

Here, reuse the "petmapper.xml" file created in Example-1. Add the following XML to the "petmapper.xml" file.

```
<select id="callPetOwnerFunction" parameterType="java.util.Map"
        resultType="java.util.Map" statementType="CALLABLE">
    { #{owner, javaType=String, jdbcType=VARCHAR, mode=OUT} = call
    get_pet_owner(#{name, javaType=String, jdbcType=VARCHAR, mode=IN}) }
</select>
```

NOTE: Make sure the complete call statement is in one line. You can see the following exception if you break the SQL statement in two lines.

```
### The error occurred while setting parameters
### SQL: { ? = call get_pet_owner(?) }
### Cause: java.sql.SQLException: Malformed SQL92 string at position: 3.
Expecting "=" got "
```

Step 5: Create a DAO class and its implementation.

The `PetDAO` interface contains methods used for executing stored functions. The complete interface definition is provided below.

```java
// PetDAO.java
package com.learning.spring.db.mybatis;

import java.util.List;

public interface PetDAO {

    void callPetOwnerFunction();
}
```

The `PetDAOImpl` class implements the above specified methods. The complete class code is provided below.

```java
// PetDAOImpl.java
package com.learning.spring.db.mybatis;

import org.mybatis.spring.SqlSessionTemplate;
import java.util.*;

public class PetDAOImpl implements PetDAO {

    private SqlSessionTemplate sqlSessionTemplate;

    public void callPetOwnerFunction() {
        HashMap<String,String> inputMap = new HashMap<String,String>();
        inputMap.put("name", "Slim");
        inputMap.put("owner", "");

        sqlSessionTemplate.selectOne("callPetOwnerFunction", inputMap);

        // Printing the output on console
        System.out.println("--- Function result owner ---" +
                inputMap.get("owner"));
    }
}
```

Step 6: Create a main class to test the code.

Listing 4-3 provides the complete class code; run the following stand-alone class to view the output on console.

Listing 4-3: Stand-alone class to test the stored function

```java
// MyBatisTestStoredProcedures.java
package com.learning.db.mybatis;

import org.springframework.context.support.
                ClassPathXmlApplicationContext;
import java.util.List;

public class MyBatisTestStoredProcedures {

    public static void main(String[] args) {
```

```
        try {
            ClassPathXmlApplicationContext appContext =
                new ClassPathXmlApplicationContext(new String[]
                    {"applicationContext-myBatis.xml"});

            PetDAO petDAOImpl = (PetDAO)
                        appContext.getBean("petDAOImpl");

            petDAOImpl.callPetOwnerFunction();

        } catch (Exception ex) {
            ex.printStackTrace();
        }
    }
}
```

Executing Stored Procedures (Annotation-based Approach)

This section illustrates the Annotation-based approach for executing stored procedures.

Example 5: How to Execute Stored Procedures – CURSOR Parameters

How to execute database stored procedures using MyBatis-provided annotations is illustrated in this example. Here, reuse the stored procedure "read_all_pets" created in the previous example. This "read_all_pets(...)" stored procedure returns the list of records.

The steps required to implement this example are listed below.

1. Create a data value object (DVO) class.
2. Create a MyBatis-specific "java-mybatis-config.xml" file.
3. Create a "petmapperdata.xml" file.
4. Create a pet mapper class.
5. Create a DAO class and its implementation.
6. Create a main class to test the code.

The preceding steps are described in the following sections:

Step 1: Create a data value object (DVO) class.

Here, reuse the PetDVO class created in previous example.

Step 2: Create a MyBatis-specific "java-mybatis-config.xml" file.

This file contains database-specific environment settings and other MyBatis-specific required configurations. The complete XML file is provided below and is named the "java-mybatis-config.xml".

```
<?xml version="1.0" encoding="UTF-8" ?>
<!DOCTYPE configuration PUBLIC "-//mybatis.org//DTD Config 3.0//EN"
"http://mybatis.org/dtd/mybatis-3-config.dtd">
```

```
<configuration>

    <settings>
        <setting name="cacheEnabled" value="true"/>
        <setting name="lazyLoadingEnabled" value="true"/>
        <setting name="multipleResultSetsEnabled" value="true"/>
        <setting name="useColumnLabel" value="true"/>
        <setting name="useGeneratedKeys" value="false"/>
        <setting name="defaultExecutorType" value="SIMPLE"/>
        <setting name="defaultStatementTimeout" value="100"/>
    </settings>

    <typeAliases>
        <typeAlias alias="PetDVO"
                   type="com.learning.db.mybatis.PetDVO"/>
    </typeAliases>

    <environments default="development">
        <environment id="development">
            <transactionManager type="JDBC"/>
            <dataSource type="POOLED">
                <property name="driver"
                          value="oracle.jdbc.OracleDriver"/>
                <property name="url"
                    value="jdbc:oracle:thin:@localhost:1521:xe"/>
                <property name="username" value="SPOWNER"/>
                <property name="password" value="PASSWORD"/>
            </dataSource>
        </environment>
    </environments>

    <mappers>
        <mapper resource="petmapperdata.xml"/>
    </mappers>

</configuration>
```

Step 3: Create a "petmapperdata.xml" file.

In this example, "petmapperdata.xml" file is used to configure the re-usable cursor result map definition. This result map can be re-used in XML and Annotation-based approaches. The complete XML file is provided below and is named the "petmapperdata.xml".

```
<?xml version="1.0" encoding="UTF-8" ?>
<!DOCTYPE mapper PUBLIC "-//mybatis.org//DTD Mapper 3.0//EN"
        "http://mybatis.org/dtd/mybatis-3-mapper.dtd">

<mapper namespace="petmapper">

    <resultMap id="cursorData" type="PetDVO">
        <result property="sex" column="sex"/>
        <result property="name" column="name"/>
        <result property="owner" column="owner"/>
        <result property="species" column="species"/>
        <result property="birth" column="birth"/>
        <result property="death" column="death"/>
```

```
        </resultMap>

</mapper>
```

Step 4: Create a pet mapper class.

MyBatis provided `@Select`, `@Insert`, `@Update`, and `@Delete` annotations can be used for executing stored procedures. The complete mapper interface code is provided below.

```java
// PetMapper.java
package com.learning.db.mybatis.java;

import org.apache.ibatis.annotations.*;
import org.apache.ibatis.mapping.StatementType;
import com.learning.db.mybatis.PetDVO;

import java.util.*;

public interface PetMapper {

    @Select(value = " { CALL read_all_pets( " +
             " #{petData, mode=OUT, jdbcType=CURSOR,
             javaType=ResultSet, resultMap=cursorData} )} ")
    @Options(statementType = StatementType.CALLABLE)
    public List<PetDVO> callReadAllPets(HashMap<String,
                                        List<PetDVO>> inputMap);
}
```

Let us review the SQL statement.

- select → used for executing the select statements.
- petData → list of domain objects.
- mode → represents the OUT variable.
- jdbcType → represents database procedure output type.
- javaType → represents the mapping output type in Java.
- cursorData → result map mapping definition specified in mapper XML file.

Step 5: Create a DAO class and its implementation.

The `PetDAOImpl` class implements the above-specified method. The complete class code is provided below.

```java
// PetDAOImpl.java
package com.learning.db.mybatis.java;

import org.apache.ibatis.session.SqlSession;
import org.apache.ibatis.session.SqlSessionFactory;
import org.apache.ibatis.session.SqlSessionFactoryBuilder;
import org.apache.ibatis.io.Resources;

import java.io.InputStream;
import java.util.*;

import com.learning.db.mybatis.PetDVO;
```

```
public class PetDAOImpl {

    private static SqlSession getSqlSession() throws Exception {
        String resource = "java-mybatis-config.xml";
        InputStream inputStream =
                Resources.getResourceAsStream(resource);
        SqlSessionFactory sqlSessionFactory =
            new SqlSessionFactoryBuilder().build(inputStream);
        sqlSessionFactory.getConfiguration().
                    addMapper(PetMapper.class);
        return sqlSessionFactory.openSession();
    }

    public List<PetDVO> callReadAllPets() throws Exception {
        SqlSession sqlSession = getSqlSession();
        PetMapper mapper = sqlSession.getMapper(PetMapper.class);

        HashMap<String, List<PetDVO>> inputMap =
                        new HashMap<String, List<PetDVO>>();
        List<PetDVO> petList = new ArrayList<PetDVO>();
        inputMap.put("petData", petList);

        mapper.callReadAllPets(inputMap);
        List<PetDVO> outputData = inputMap.get("petData");
        return outputData;
    }
}
```

Step 6: Create a main class to test the code.

Listing 4-4 provides the complete class code; run the following stand-alone class to view the output on console.

Listing 4-4: Stand-alone class to test the stored procedure

```
// JavaMyBatisMain.java
package com.learning.db.mybatis.java;

import java.util.*;
import com.learning.db.mybatis.PetDVO;

public class JavaMyBatisMain {

    public static void main(String[] args) {
        try {
            JavaMyBatisMain main = new JavaMyBatisMain();
            main.selectAllPets();
        } catch (Exception ex) {
            ex.printStackTrace();
        }
    }

    private void callReadAllPets() throws Exception {
        PetDAOImpl petDAOImpl = new PetDAOImpl();
        List<PetDVO> outputData = petDAOImpl.callReadAllPets();
        System.out.println("--- outputData ---" + outputData);
    }
```

```
}
```

Example 6: How to Execute Stored Procedures –IN and OUT Parameters

Here, reuse the stored procedure "read_pet" created in Example-1. This "read_pet(...)" stored procedure has one IN parameter and five OUT parameters. This procedure returns the data in OUT parameters for a given input.

The steps required to implement this example are listed below.

1. Create a data value object (DVO) class.
2. Create a MyBatis-specific "java-mybatis-config.xml" file.
3. Create a pet mapper class.
4. Create a DAO class and its implementation.
5. Create a main class to test the code.

The preceding steps are described in the following sections:

Step 1: Create a data value object (DVO) class.

Here, reuse the `PetDVO` class created in previous examples.

Step 2: Create a MyBatis-specific "java-mybatis-config.xml" file.

Here, reuse the "java-mybatis-config.xml" file created in previous example. The following XML elements are not needed; MyBatis annotations are used in this example.

```
<typeAliases>
    <typeAlias alias="PetDVO" type="com.learning.db.mybatis.PetDVO"/>
</typeAliases>

<mappers>
    <mapper resource="petmapperdata.xml"/>
</mappers>
```

Step 3: Create a pet mapper class.

Here, reuse the `PetMapper` interface created in previous example. Add the following method to the `PetMapper` interface.

```
@Select(value = " { CALL read_pet(   " +
    "     #{name, mode=IN, jdbcType=VARCHAR},      " +
    "     #{owner, mode=OUT, jdbcType=VARCHAR},    " +
    "     #{species, mode=OUT, jdbcType=VARCHAR}," +
    "     #{sex, mode=OUT, jdbcType=VARCHAR},      " +
    "     #{birth, mode=OUT, jdbcType=DATE},       " +
    "     #{death, mode=OUT, jdbcType=DATE}        " +
    " )} ")
@Options(statementType = StatementType.CALLABLE)
public void callReadPet(PetDVO petDVO);
```

Step 4: Create a DAO class and its implementation.

Here, reuse the `PetDAOImpl` class created in previous example. Add the following method to the `PetDAOImpl` class.

```java
public void callReadPet(PetDVO petDVO) throws Exception {
    SqlSession sqlSession = getSqlSession();
    PetMapper mapper = sqlSession.getMapper(PetMapper.class);

    mapper.callReadPet(petDVO);
}
```

Step 5: Create a main class to test the code.

Listing 4-5 provides the complete class code; run the following stand-alone class to view the output on the console.

Listing 4-5: Stand-alone class to test the stored procedure

```java
// JavaMyBatisMain.java
package com.learning.db.mybatis.java;

import java.util.*;
import com.learning.db.mybatis.PetDVO;

public class JavaMyBatisMain {

    public static void main(String[] args) {
        try {
            JavaMyBatisMain main = new JavaMyBatisMain();
            main.selectAllPets();
        } catch (Exception ex) {
            ex.printStackTrace();
        }
    }

    private void callReadPet() throws Exception {
        PetDAOImpl petDAOImpl = new PetDAOImpl();
        PetDVO petDVO = new PetDVO();
        petDVO.setName("Slimmy");

        petDAOImpl.callReadPet(petDVO);
        System.out.println(" Proc Output :" + petDVO);
    }
}
```

Using XML and Annotations (Combined Approach)

We have discussed both XML and Annotation-based approaches for executing SQL statements and database stored procedures. It is possible to combine both XML and annotation-based approaches. Example -5 uses the combined approach for executing stored procedures. Also, it is possible to eliminate the XML completely and use only the MyBatis-provided Java API for executing the SQL statements. There is no hard-and-fast rule approach to be used in your application. This is completely depends on developer's comfort, the application need, and their prior experience with the framework.

Summary

This section summarizes the features provided by the MyBatis framework for executing database stored procedures and functions.

- MyBatis provided `@Select, @Insert, @Delete,` and `@Update` annotations can be used for executing stored procedures and functions.
- `@Options(statementType=StatementType.CALLABLE)` is the valid statement type used for executing stored procedures and functions.

Chapter 5. MyBatis-Spring Transaction Management

Spring framework provides a transaction management API to manage transactions for Java-based applications. Spring provides a consistent transaction management framework that can be used with any data access framework such as Spring-JDBC, Hibernate, MyBatis, and so forth. The spring transaction framework is an alternative to the EJB-provided container managed entity bean transaction model. However, the spring transaction framework does not require an application server to manage the transactions.

This chapter will discuss the following topics:

- MyBatis-Spring declarative transaction management
- MyBatis-Spring programmatic transaction management
- MyBatis-Spring annotation-based transaction management
- Spring transaction attributes and their use

Advantages of Spring Transactions

- Spring provides a simple AOP-based configuration to manage the transaction behavior of methods.
- Spring provides annotation and API-based programming models to manage transactions.
- Spring provides support for both declarative and programmatic transaction management.
- Spring provides support for standalone and JNDI-based data sources and it functions in any environment.
- It is a simple and consistent programming model that supports various data access frameworks such as Spring-JDBC, Hibernate, MyBatis, and JPA.
- An application server is not needed to manage the transactions; spring can be used in any standalone environment.

Declarative and Programmatic Transaction Management

Spring provides support for both declarative and programmatic transaction management. In the case of declarative transaction management, spring provides AOP-based XML configurations to manage the transaction behavior. The spring declarative transaction behavior can be applied to any class or interface method without modifying the application code. The benefit of this approach is that the application code does not depend on spring's API and looks cleaner.

In the case of programmatic transaction management, spring's API is used to manage the transactions. Spring also offers the annotation-based programming approach to manage transactions. This chapter illustrates the capabilities of both declarative and programmatic transaction management.

Transaction Propagation in EJB and Spring

This section illustrates the purpose of transaction attributes in EJB and spring. EJB supports the following six transaction attributes. A transaction attribute specifies how the container must manage the transaction when a client invokes a method of an EJB component.

- REQUIRED
- REQUIRESNEW
- MANDATORY
- SUPPORTS
- NOT SUPPORTED
- NEVER

The following table summarizes the significance of each transaction attribute in EJB.

Transaction Attribute	Invoking client has transaction	Invoking client does not have transaction
REQUIRED	Transaction is propagated	New transaction will be started.
REQUIRESNEW	Suspends the current transaction; starts a new transaction	Starts a new transaction
MANDATORY	Propagates the current transaction.	Throws a `TransactionRequiredException`
SUPPORTS	Propagates the current transaction.	
NOT SUPPORTED	Suspends the current transaction.	
NEVER	Throws `RemoteException`	

Similarly, the following transaction attributes are used in the spring framework to control transaction propagation.

- REQUIRED
- REQUIRESNEW
- NESTED

In spring, the REQUIRED and REQUIRESNEW transaction attributes function the same as they do in EJB. The NESTED transaction attribute is used for a single transaction that has multiple save points and allows the transaction to rollback to the specified save point.

Demo Examples

Example 1: AOP-based Declarative Transaction Management

This example illustrates the configurations required to handle declarative transactions. The steps required to implement this example are listed below.

1. Create a DAO interface and its implementation class
2. Create a data value object (DVO) class
3. Create a mapper file and MyBatis configuration files
4. Configure the datasource and transaction manager in an application context file.
5. Create a main class to test the code.

The above-specified steps are described in the following sections.

Step 1: Create a DAO interface and its implementation class

The definition of the PetDAO interface is provided below. This interface has "insert" and "delete" methods.

```
// PetDAO.java
package com.learning.db.mybatis.tx.dao;

import java.util.List;

public interface PetDAO {

    public void doInsertAndUpdateInTx();

    public void insertPet(PetDVO petDVO);

    public void updatePetData(PetDVO petDVO);
}
```

The above-specified interface methods are implemented in the PetDAOImpl class. The doInsertAndUpdateInTx() method is used to wrap the "insert" and "update" methods and is executed in one transaction. If an exception occurs in this method, it has to rollback both the "insert" and "update" operations. The doInsertAndUpdateInTx() method code is provided below.

```
public void doInsertAndUpdateInTx() {
    insertPet(petDVO);
    updatePetData(petDataObj);
}
```

Let us modify the above method slightly to create an exception between "insert" and "update". The following code throws a divide-by-zero exception. In this scenario, the "insert" operation will rollback autiomatically.

```
public void doInsertAndUpdateInTx() {
    insertPet(petDVO);

    // create an error
    int i = 0;
    int j = 100 / i;

    updatePetData(petDataObj);
}
```

The complete class code is provided below.

```java
// PetDAOImpl.java
package com.learning.db.mybatis.tx.dao;

import org.springframework.jdbc.core.JdbcTemplate;
import org.springframework.transaction.TransactionStatus;

import java.util.*;
import java.sql.Types;

public class PetDAOImpl implements PetDAO {

    private SqlSessionTemplate sqlSessionTemplate;

    public void doInsertAndUpdateInTx() {
        try {
            // Insert a record
            insertPet();

            // Create an error to get the exception
            int i = 0;
            int j = 100 / i;

            // Update pet data
            updatePetData();

        } catch (Exception ex) {
            TransactionStatus status =
                    TransactionAspectSupport.currentTransactionStatus();
            System.out.println(" --- is Completed --- " +
                                    status.isCompleted());
            status.setRollbackOnly();
        }
    }

    public void insertPet() {
        // Data to be inserted
        PetDVO petDVO = new PetDVO();
        petDVO.setName("Slim1");
        petDVO.setOwner("Steve");
        petDVO.setSpecies("Snake");
        petDVO.setSex("f");
        petDVO.setBirth(new Date());

        HashMap<String, Object> inputMap =
                        new HashMap<String, Object>();
        inputMap.put("name", petDVO.getName());
        inputMap.put("owner", petDVO.getOwner() );
        inputMap.put("species", petDVO.getSpecies() );
        inputMap.put("sex", petDVO.getSex());
        inputMap.put("birth", petDVO.getBirth());
        inputMap.put("death", petDVO.getDeath());

        sqlSessionTemplate.insert("createPet", inputMap);
    }

    public void updatePetData() {
```

```
            // Updating the data
            PetDVO petDVO = new PetDVO();
            petDVO.setName("Slimmy");
            petDVO.setSex("f");
            petDVO.setBirth(new Date());

            HashMap<String, Object> inputMap
                             = new HashMap<String, Object>();
            inputMap.put("birth", petDVO.getBirth());
            inputMap.put("sex", petDVO.getSex());
            inputMap.put("name", petDVO.getName());

            sqlSessionTemplate.update("updatePetData", inputMap);
        }

    public void setSqlSessionTemplate(SqlSessionTemplate
                        sqlSessionTemplate) {
            this.sqlSessionTemplate = sqlSessionTemplate;
        }
}
```

Step 2: Create a data value object (DVO) class

The following domain object is used.

```
// PetDVO.java
package com.learning.spring.tx.dao;

import java.util.Date;
import java.io.Serializable;

public class PetDVO implements Serializable {

    private String name;
    private String owner;
    private String species;
    private String sex;
    private Date birth;
    private Date death;

    // Add getter and setter methods
}
```

Step 3: Create a mapper file and MyBatis configuration files

This file contains database-specific SQL statements. The complete mapper XML file is provided below and is named the "petmappertx.xml".

```
<?xml version="1.0" encoding="UTF-8" ?>
<!DOCTYPE mapper PUBLIC "-//mybatis.org//DTD Mapper 3.0//EN"
            "http://mybatis.org/dtd/mybatis-3-mapper.dtd">

<mapper namespace="petmapper">

    <insert id="createPet" parameterType="java.util.Map">
        <selectKey keyProperty="id" resultType="int" order="BEFORE">
```

```
                SELECT PET_ID_SEQ.nextval AS id FROM dual
         </selectKey>

         INSERT INTO Pet (ID, NAME, OWNER, SPECIES, SEX, BIRTH)
         VALUES (#{id}, #{name}, #{owner}, #{species}, #{sex}, #{birth})
     </insert>

     <update id="updatePetData" parameterType="java.util.Map">
         UPDATE Pet p
         SET p.birth = #{birth},
         p.sex = #{sex}
         WHERE p.name = #{name}
     </update>

</mapper>
```

Configure mapper XML file and other MyBatis-specific configurations. The complete XML file is provided below and is named the "sqlMapConfigTx.xml".

```xml
<?xml version="1.0" encoding="UTF-8" ?>
<!DOCTYPE configuration PUBLIC "-//mybatis.org//DTD Config 3.0//EN"
"http://mybatis.org/dtd/mybatis-3-config.dtd">

<configuration>

    <settings>
        <setting name="cacheEnabled" value="true"/>
        <setting name="lazyLoadingEnabled" value="true"/>
        <setting name="multipleResultSetsEnabled" value="true"/>
        <setting name="useColumnLabel" value="true"/>
        <setting name="useGeneratedKeys" value="false"/>
        <setting name="defaultExecutorType" value="SIMPLE"/>
        <setting name="defaultStatementTimeout" value="100"/>
    </settings>

    <typeAliases>
        <typeAlias alias="PetDVO"
                     type="com.learning.db.mybatis.PetDVO"/>
    </typeAliases>

    <mappers>
        <mapper resource="petmappertx.xml"/>
    </mappers>

</configuration>
```

Step 4: Configure the datasource and transaction manager in an application context file.

The spring application context file is used to configure the datasource, transaction manager, SQL session template, and data access objects. The complete application context XML file is provided below and is named the "applicationContext-tx.xml"

```xml
<?xml version="1.0" encoding="UTF-8"?>
<beans xmlns="http://www.springframework.org/schema/beans"
     xmlns:xsi="http://www.w3.org/2001/XMLSchema-instance"
     xmlns:context="http://www.springframework.org/schema/context"
```

```xml
xmlns:aop="http://www.springframework.org/schema/aop"
xmlns:tx="http://www.springframework.org/schema/tx"
xsi:schemaLocation="http://www.springframework.org/schema/beans
    http://www.springframework.org/schema/beans/
                spring-beans-3.0.xsd
    http://www.springframework.org/schema/context
    http://www.springframework.org/schema/context/
                spring-context-3.0.xsd
    http://www.springframework.org/schema/tx
    http://www.springframework.org/schema/tx/spring-tx-3.0.xsd
    http://www.springframework.org/schema/aop
    http://www.springframework.org/schema/aop/spring-aop-3.0.xsd ">

<bean id="dataSource" class="org.springframework.jdbc.
                    datasource.DriverManagerDataSource">
    <property name="driverClassName">
        <value>oracle.jdbc.OracleDriver</value>
    </property>
    <property name="url">
        <value>jdbc:oracle:thin:@localhost:1521:xe</value>
    </property>
    <property name="username">
        <value>SPOWNER</value>
    </property>
    <property name="password">
        <value>PASSWORD</value>
    </property>
</bean>

<!-- Transaction manager for the data source -->
<bean id="txManager" class="org.springframework.jdbc.datasource.
        DataSourceTransactionManager">
    <property name="dataSource" ref="dataSource"/>
</bean>

<bean id="sqlSessionFactory" class="org.mybatis.spring.
                            SqlSessionFactoryBean">
    <property name="dataSource" ref="dataSource"/>
    <property name="configLocation" value="sqlMapConfigTx.xml" />
</bean>

<bean id="sqlSessionTemplate" class="org.mybatis.spring.
                            SqlSessionTemplate">
    <constructor-arg index="0" ref="sqlSessionFactory"/>
</bean>

<bean id="petDAOImpl" class="com.learning.db.mybatis.tx.dao.
                            PetDAOImpl">
    <property name="sqlSessionTemplate" ref="sqlSessionTemplate"/>
</bean>

<aop:config>
    <aop:pointcut id="petDaoOperation"
            expression="execution(* com.learning.db.mybatis.tx.
                            dao.PetDAO.*(..))"/>
    <aop:advisor pointcut-ref="petDaoOperation"
                advice-ref="txAdvice"/>
```

```
        </aop:config>

        <tx:advice id="txAdvice" transaction-manager="txManager">
            <tx:attributes>
                <tx:method name="get*" read-only="true"/>
                <tx:method name="*"/>
            </tx:attributes>
        </tx:advice>
</beans>
```

A pointcut expression is represented in AspectJ expression language. Let us review the pointcut expressions provided below, the first of which executes the `addPet()` method.

```
execution(* com.learning.db.mybatis.tx.dao.PetDAO.addPet(..))
```

The following pointcut expression executes any method defined in the `PetService` interface.

```
execution(* com.learning.db.mybatis.tx.service.PetService.*(..))
```

The following pointcut expression executes any method defined in the `service` package.

```
execution(* com.learning.db.mybatis.tx.service.*.*(..))
```

Step 5: Create a main class to test the code.

Listing 5-1 provides the complete class code; run the following stand-alone class to view the output.

Listing 5-1: Stand-alone class used for testing

```
// TxMain.java
package com.learning.spring.tx;

import org.springframework.context.support.
            ClassPathXmlApplicationContext;
import org.springframework.context.ApplicationContext;
import com.learning.spring.tx.dao.PetDAO;

public class TxMain {

    public static void main(final String[] args) throws Exception {
        ApplicationContext ctx = new ClassPathXmlApplicationContext(
                new String [] {"applicationContext-tx.xml"});
        PetDAO petDAO = (PetDAO) ctx.getBean("petDAOImpl");
        petDAO.doInsertAndUpdateInTx();
    }
}
```

Example 2: Programmatic Transaction Management

This example illustrates management of transactions programmatically using Spring API. In this example Spring-provided `TransactionTemplate` class is used to manage the transactions. The steps required to implement this example are listed below.

1. Create a DAO interface and its implementation class
2. Create a data value object (DVO) class
3. Create a mapper file and MyBatis configuration files
4. Configure the datasource and transaction manager in an application context file.
5. Create a main class to test the code.

The above-specified steps are described in the following sections:

Step 1: Create a DAO interface and its implementation class

Here, reuse the `PetDAO` and `PetDAOImpl` classes created in Example-1. Add the following method to the `PetDAO` interface.

```
public interface PetDAO {
    void doInsertAndUpdateUsingTxTemplate();
}
```

Here, reuse the `PetDAOImpl` class created in Example-1 with the following change. The complete class code is provided below.

```
// PetDAOImpl
package com.learning.db.mybatis.tx.dao;

@Component
public class PetDAOImpl implements PetDAO {

    private SqlSessionTemplate sqlSessionTemplate;

    private TransactionTemplate transactionTemplate;

    public void doInsertAndUpdateUsingTxTemplate() {
        transactionTemplate.execute(
                new TransactionCallbackWithoutResult() {
            protected void doInTransactionWithoutResult(
                    TransactionStatus status) {
                try {
                    // Insert a record
                    insertPet();

                    // Create an error to get the exception
                    int i = 0;
                    int j = 100 / i;

                    // Update a record
                    updatePetData();

                } catch (Exception ex) {
                    System.out.println(" is Completed " +
                            status.isCompleted());
                    status.setRollbackOnly();
                }
            }
        });
    }
```

```
    public void insertPet() {
        // Reuse the code from Example-1
    }

    public void updatePetData() {
        // Reuse the code from Example-1
    }

    public void setTransactionTemplate(TransactionTemplate
                transactionTemplate) {
        this.transactionTemplate = transactionTemplate;
    }

    public void setSqlSessionTemplate(SqlSessionTemplate
                sqlSessionTemplate) {
        this.sqlSessionTemplate = sqlSessionTemplate;
    }
}
```

Spring provides the `TransactionTemplate` class to execute the methods in a transaction. The `status.setRollbackOnly()` method rolls back the transaction if any exception occurs within the scope of a transaction. The complete method code is provided below.

```
public void doInsertAndUpdateUsingTxTemplate() {

    transactionTemplate.execute(new TransactionCallbackWithoutResult() {
        protected void doInTransactionWithoutResult(
                    TransactionStatus status) {
            try {
                // Insert a record
                insertPet();

                // Create an error to get the exception
                int i = 0;
                int j = 100/i;

                // Update a record
                updatePetData();

            } catch (Exception ex) {
                // Printing the transaction status
                System.out.println("--- is Completed ---" +
                        status.isCompleted());
                status.setRollbackOnly();
            }
        }
    });
}
```

Step 2: Create a data value object (DVO) class.

Here, reuse the `PetDVO` class created in Example -1.

Step 3: Create a mapper file and MyBatis configuration files

Here, reuse the files created in Example -1.

Step 4: Configure the datasource and transaction manager in an application context file.

The spring application context file is used to configure the datasource, transaction manager, spring JDBC template, transaction template, and DAO classes. The complete application context XML file is provided below and is named the "applicationContext-tx-template.xml".

```xml
<?xml version="1.0" encoding="UTF-8"?>
<beans xmlns="http://www.springframework.org/schema/beans"
    xmlns:xsi="http://www.w3.org/2001/XMLSchema-instance"
    xmlns:context="http://www.springframework.org/schema/context"
    xsi:schemaLocation="http://www.springframework.org/schema/beans
    http://www.springframework.org/schema/beans/spring-beans-3.0.xsd
    http://www.springframework.org/schema/context
    http://www.springframework.org/schema/context/
                spring-context-3.0.xsd">

    <!-- Configure datasource -->
    <bean id="dataSource" class="org.springframework.jdbc.datasource.
                DriverManagerDataSource">
        <property name="driverClassName">
            <value>oracle.jdbc.OracleDriver</value>
        </property>
        <property name="url">
            <value>jdbc:oracle:thin:@localhost:1521:xe</value>
        </property>
        <property name="username">
            <value>SPOWNER</value>
        </property>
        <property name="password">
            <value>PASSWORD</value>
        </property>
    </bean>

    <!-- Transaction manager for the data source -->
    <bean id="txManager" class="org.springframework.jdbc.datasource.
                DataSourceTransactionManager">
        <property name="dataSource" ref="dataSource"/>
    </bean>

    <!-- Configure the SqlSessionFactory -->
    <bean id="sqlSessionFactory"
            class="org.mybatis.spring.SqlSessionFactoryBean">
        <property name="dataSource" ref="dataSource"/>
        <property name="configLocation" value="sqlMapConfigTx.xml" />
    </bean>

    <!-- Configure the SqlSessionTemplate -->
    <bean id="sqlSessionTemplate"
        class="org.mybatis.spring.SqlSessionTemplate">
        <constructor-arg index="0" ref="sqlSessionFactory"/>
    </bean>

    <!-- Configure Spring TransactionTemplate class -->
    <bean id="transactionTemplate" class="org.springframework.
                transaction.support.TransactionTemplate">
        <property name="transactionManager" ref="txManager"/>
    </bean>
```

```
<!--Injecting TransactionTemplate and SQLSessionTemplate into DAO-->
<bean id="petDAOImpl" class="com.learning.db.mybatis.
            tx.dao.PetDAOImpl">
    <property name="sqlSessionTemplate" ref="sqlSessionTemplate"/>
    <property name="transactionTemplate"
            ref="transactionTemplate"/>
</bean>

</beans>
```

Step 5: Create a main class to test the code.

Listing 5-2 provides the complete class code; run the following stand-alone class to view the output.

Listing 5-2: Stand-alone class used for testing

```
// TxMain.java
package com.learning.spring.tx;

import org.springframework.context.support.
            ClassPathXmlApplicationContext;
import org.springframework.context.ApplicationContext;
import com.learning.spring.tx.dao.PetDAO;

public class TxMain {

    public static void main(final String[] args) throws Exception {
        ApplicationContext ctx = new ClassPathXmlApplicationContext(new
                String [] { "applicationContext-tx-template.xml" });
        PetDAO petDAO = (PetDAO) ctx.getBean("petDAOImpl");
        petDAO.doInsertAndUpdateUsingTxTemplate();
    }
}
```

Transaction Management Using Spring Annotations

The `@Transactional` annotation with `<tx:annotation-driven>` XML configuration provides the transactional behavior to the annotated methods. The `@Transactional` annotation is used to specify the metadata required for the runtime infrastructure in managing transactions. This annotation can be used with interfaces, methods of an interface, classes, and methods of a class. The `<tx:annotation-driven>` element enables the annotation-based transactional behavior, and this tag looks for only `@Transactional`-annotated methods or classes.

The following XML element enables the annotation-based transaction behavior.

```
<tx:annotation-driven transaction-manager="txManager"/>
```

The default `@Transactional`-annotation properties are listed below.

- Transaction Propagation = REQUIRED
- Isolation level = DEFAULT
- Rollback-for = any runtime exception triggers a transaction rollback.

The following code demonstrates the use of `@Transactional`-annotation.

```
@Transactional(readOnly = false)
public void doInsertAndUpdateInTx() {

    // Insert a record
    insertPet(PetDVO petDVO);

    // Update a record
    updatePetData(PetDVO petDVO);
}
```

Example 3: Annotation-based Transaction Management

This example illustrates programmatic handling of transactions using spring annotations. The steps required to implement this example are listed below.

1. Create a DAO interface and its implementation class
2. Create a data value object (DVO) class
3. Create a mapper file and MyBatis configuration files
4. Configure the datasource and transaction manager in an application context file.
5. Create a main class to test the code.

The above-specified steps are described in the following sections:

Step 1: Create a DAO interface and its implementation class

Here, reuse the `PetDAO` and `PetDAOImpl` classes created in Example -1. The `@Transactional`-annotated method is executed in a transaction. The annotated method signature is provided below.

```
@Transactional(readOnly = false)
public void doInsertAndUpdateInTx() {
    PetDVO petDVO = new PetDVO();
    petDVO.setName("Slim1");
    petDVO.setOwner("Steve");
    petDVO.setSpecies("Snake");
    petDVO.setSex("f");
    petDVO.setBirth(new Date());

    // Insert a record
    insertPet(petDVO);

    // Create an error to get the exception
    int i = 0;
    int j = 100 / i;

    PetDVO petDataObj = new PetDVO();
    petDataObj.setName("Slimmy");
    petDataObj.setSex("m");
    petDataObj.setBirth(new Date());

    // Update a record
    updatePetData();
```

}

Step 2: Create data value object (DVO) class

Here, reuse the `PetDVO` class created in Example -1.

Step 3: Create a mapper file and MyBatis configuration files

Here, reuse the files created in Example -1.

Step 4: Configure the datasource and transaction manager in an application context file.

The complete application context XML file is provided below and is named the "applicationContext-tx-annotations.xml".

```xml
<?xml version="1.0" encoding="UTF-8"?>
<beans xmlns="http://www.springframework.org/schema/beans"
    xmlns:xsi="http://www.w3.org/2001/XMLSchema-instance"
    xmlns:context="http://www.springframework.org/schema/context"
    xmlns:tx="http://www.springframework.org/schema/tx"
    xsi:schemaLocation="http://www.springframework.org/schema/beans
    http://www.springframework.org/schema/beans/spring-beans-3.0.xsd
    http://www.springframework.org/schema/context
    http://www.springframework.org/schema/context/spring-context-3.0.xsd
    http://www.springframework.org/schema/tx
    http://www.springframework.org/schema/tx/spring-tx-3.0.xsd ">

    <bean id="myDataSource" class="org.springframework.jdbc.datasource.
                        DriverManagerDataSource">
        <property name="driverClassName">
            <value>oracle.jdbc.OracleDriver</value>
        </property>
        <property name="url">
            <value>jdbc:oracle:thin:@localhost:1521:xe</value>
        </property>
        <property name="username">
            <value>SPOWNER</value>
        </property>
        <property name="password">
            <value>PASSWORD</value>
        </property>
    </bean>

    <!-- Transaction manager for the data source -->
    <bean id="txManager" class="org.springframework.jdbc.datasource.
                DataSourceTransactionManager">
        <property name="dataSource" ref="myDataSource"/>
    </bean>

    <!-- Enable the annotation-based transaction behavior -->
    <tx:annotation-driven transaction-manager="txManager"/>

    <bean id="sqlSessionFactory" class="org.mybatis.spring.
                                    SqlSessionFactoryBean">
        <property name="dataSource" ref="dataSource"/>
        <property name="configLocation" value="sqlMapConfigTx.xml"/>
```

```xml
        </bean>

                .
        <bean id="sqlSessionTemplate" class="org.mybatis.spring.
                                            SqlSessionTemplate">
            <constructor-arg index="0" ref="sqlSessionFactory"/>
        </bean>

        <bean id="petDAOImpl" class="com.learning.db.mybatis.tx.
                                annotations.PetDAOImpl">
            <property name="sqlSessionTemplate" ref="sqlSessionTemplate"/>
        </bean>

</beans>
```

Step 4: Create a main class to test the code.

Listing 5-3 provides the complete class code; run the following stand-alone class to view the output.

Listing 5-3: Stand-alone class used for testing

```java
// TxMain.java
package com.learning.spring.tx;

import org.springframework.context.support.
            ClassPathXmlApplicationContext;
import org.springframework.context.ApplicationContext;
import com.learning.spring.tx.dao.PetDAO;

public class TxMain {

    public static void main(final String[] args) throws Exception {
        ApplicationContext ctx = new ClassPathXmlApplicationContext(new
            String [] { "applicationContext-tx-annotations.xml" });
        PetDAO petDAO = (PetDAO) ctx.getBean("petDAOImpl");
        petDAO.doInsertAndUpdateInTx ();
    }
}
```

Summary

This section summarizes the features of the spring transaction framework.

- Spring provides the `TransactionTemplate` class to execute the methods in a transaction. The `status.setRollbackOnly()` method rolls back the transaction if an exception occurs within the scope of a transaction.
- The `@Transactional` annotation with `<tx:annotation-driven>` XML configuration provides the transactional behavior to the annotated methods.
- The supported spring transaction propagation attributes are REQUIRED, REQUIRESNEW and NESTED.
- The `<tx:advice>` tag is used to specify the various transaction settings.

Figure 5-1 summarizes the most important points described in this chapter.

Figure 5-1 MyBatis and Spring transaction management features.

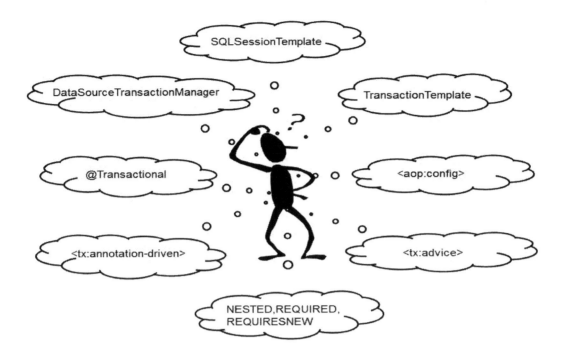

Chapter 6. MyBatis with Velocity

Velocity is an open-source template engine that provides a scripting language to reference the Java data objects. The scripting language used within Velocity is called Velocity Template Language (VTL). The VTL scripts can embed both with HTML as well as with XML code. Velocity templates can be used in the view layer to render the controller-provided model data. Velocity can also be used with any other framework, such as MyBatis, Spring-MVC, Struts, and so forth. Velocity is an open-source framework available under the Apache license.

MyBatis-Velocity is an extension that allows you to integrate MyBatis with Velocity. Velocity scripting language can be used with MyBatis to reference the input parameters and generate the dynamic SQL queries.

This chapter will discuss the following topics:

- Velocity syntax and fundamentals
- MyBatis integration with velocity
- Velocity syntax for generating SQL statements
- Executing select, Insert, delete, and update statements using MyBatis and Velocity
- Building dynamic SQL statements using MyBatis-Velocity

Prerequisite and Configuration Settings

This section illustrates the configurations required to integrate MyBatis with Velocity.

1. Make sure "Pet" table is created before executing the code examples.
2. Make sure "id" sequence number is generated if you work with Oracle database. Refer to Chapter -1 for details.
3. Add the "mybatis-velocity-1.0.jar" and "velocity-1.7.jar" in your classpath.
4. Configure the `defaultScriptingLanguage` attribute in your MyBatis configuration file.

```
<setting name="defaultScriptingLanguage" value="velocity"/>
```

5. Configure the scripting language driver alias in your MyBatis configuration file.

```
<typeAliases>
      <typeAlias alias="velocity"
                 type="org.mybatis.scripting.velocity.Driver"/>
</typeAliases>
```

Velocity Syntax and Fundamentals

The commonly used extension for a Velocity template is ".vm". This section illustrates how to reference the Java objects in Velocity templates. This section will help you to get familiar with the velocity scripting language syntax and fundamentals.

The Java code is:

```
Map<String, String> myMap = new HashMap<String, String>();
myMap.put("heading", "Learning Spring MVC");
```

The Velocity template code is:

```
Heading: $heading
```

The Java code is:

```
List<String> namesList = new ArrayList<String>();
namesList.add("MyBatis");
namesList.add("Learning");
namesList.add("Version 3.x");
request.setAttribute("namesList", namesList);
```

The Velocity template code is:

```
#foreach($name in $namesList)
    $name <br/>
#end
```

The Java code is:

```
Map<String, String> dataHashMap = new HashMap<String, String>();
dataHashMap.put("Topic1", "Java");
dataHashMap.put("Topic2", "MyBatis-Velocity");
dataHashMap.put("Topic3", "MyBatis-Spring");
request.setAttribute("dataHashMap", dataHashMap);
```

The Velocity template code is:

```
#foreach($key in $dataHashMap.keySet())
    Key is: $key
    Value is: $dataHashMap.get($key) <br/>
#end
```

The Java code is:

```
List<Account> accountDataList = new ArrayList<Account>();
Account account1 = new Account();
account1.setAccountNumber("121213");
account1.setAccountHolderName("John Smith");
account1.setBalance(99975L);
accountDataList.add(account1);

Account account2 = new Account();
account2.setAccountNumber("3434133");
account2.setAccountHolderName("John Sims");
account2.setBalance(45000L);
accountDataList.add(account2);
model.put("accountDataList", accountDataList);
```

The Velocity template code is:

```
<table>
    #foreach($account in $accountDataList)
        <tr>
            <td> $account.getAccountNumber() </td>
            <td> $account.getAccountHolderName() </td>
            <td> $account.getBalance()   </td>
        </tr>
    #end
</table>
```

The following example demonstrates the variable declaration in Velocity templates.

```
#set($name = "John Smith")
```

The Java code is:

```
Map<String, Account> accountDataMap =
                new HashMap<String, Account>();
accountDataMap.put("account1", account1);
accountDataMap.put("account2", account2);
model.put("accountDataMap", accountDataMap);
```

The Velocity template code is:

```
<table>
    #foreach($mapKey in $accountDataMap.keySet())
        #set($accountObj = $accountDataMap.get($mapKey))
        <tr>
            <td> $accountObj.getAccountNumber() </td>
            <td> $accountObj.getAccountHolderName() </td>
            <td> $accountObj.getBalance() </td>
        </tr>
    #end
</table>
```

The following example demonstrates the Velocity "if-else" condition syntax.

```
<div>
    #if($name.equals("Spring"))
        Spring
    #else
        Not a Spring
    #end
</div>
```

The following example demonstrates the Velocity "if-elseif" condition syntax.

```
<div>
    #if($name.equals("Spring"))
        Spring
    #elseif($name.equals("Security"))
        Security
    #else
```

```
        Java
    #end
</div>
```

The following example demonstrates the Velocity "parse" syntax. Parse is used to include a Velocity template inside another template.

```
#parse("demo/message.vm")
```

Velocity Tools:

Velocity tool is a simple POJO class which helps for reusing commonly used functionalities such as date tool, number tool, math tool, and so forth. The Velocity tool class avoids the redundant code in your application. The velocity tool provided common functionalities which can be reused across the application. The Velocity tools are configured in the "toolbox.xml" file. A sample toolbox configuration is provided below.

```
<?xml version="1.0"?>
<toolbox>
    <tool>
        <key>math</key>
        <scope>application</scope>
        <class>org.apache.velocity.tools.generic.MathTool</class>
    </tool>

    <tool>
        <key>dateTool</key>
        <scope>application</scope>
        <class>org.apache.velocity.tools.generic.DateTool</class>
    </tool>
</toolbox>
```

The following code snippet demonstrates the Velocity toolbox example syntax. In this example, Velocity-provided built-in tools are used, and Velocity allows us to configure custom Velocity tools.

```
<div>
    Velocity Tool: <br/>
    $dateTool.format("MM/dd/yyyy", $dob) <br/>
    $math.add(100, 200) <br/>
</div>
```

MyBatis-Velocity Syntax and Terminology

The preceding section illustrates the velocity scripting language syntax and its use with Java objects. How to reference the domain object data in mapper XML files to generate SQL statements is illustrated in this section.

The "#" symbol is used to reference the input parameters. An example SQL statement is provided below.

```
SELECT *  FROM Pet WHERE name = #{name}
```

Similarly, in velocity scripting the "@" symbol is used to reference the input parameters. An example SQL statement is provided below.

```
SELECT * FROM Pet WHERE name = @{name}
```

The "lang" attribute of the `<select>` statement can be used to specify the scripting language. An example SQL statement is provided below.

```
<select id="getPetObject" lang="velocity"> ... </select>
```

Building and Executing Dynamic SQL Statements

MyBatis-Velocity provides the following utilities and statements for building dynamic SQL statements. The use of the following statements is demonstrated in this section with examples.

- #set
- #if and #end
- #where() and #end
- #repeat and #end

The following example demonstrates the variable declaration in mapper XML file.

```
#set($sex = $_parameter.sex)
```

The following example demonstrates the use of `#if` statement in mapper XML file.

```
#if($!sex)
    AND sex =  @{sex, jdbcType=VARCHAR}
#end
```

MyBatis-velocity provides the following utility to build the dynamic SQL statements. The following example demonstrates the use of `#where` statements in mapper XML file.

```
#where()
    #in($_parameter.namesList $item "name")
        @{item}
    #end
#end
```

The preceding statement is used to build the following SQL statement. The "namesList" is a Java list that contains a list of Strings.

```
SELECT * from Pet WHERE name IN ('Slimmy', 'Jumbo');
```

MyBatis-velocity provides the following utility to build the dynamic SQL statements. The following example demonstrates the use of `#repeat` statement in mapper XML file. This is similar to `#foreach` statement.

```
#where()
    #repeat($_parameter.petList $petObj "," " " name IN (" ")")
        @{petObj.name}
```

```
    #end
#end
```

The preceding statement is used to build the following SQL statement. The "petList" is a Java list that contains a list of `PetDVO` domain objects.

```
SELECT * from Pet WHERE name IN ('Slimmy', 'Jumbo');
```

Demo Examples - MyBatis with Velocity

Example 1: Querying the Data – Building Dynamic SQL

How to execute SQL statements using the Spring-provided `SqlSessionTemplate` class is illustrated in this example. The steps required to implement this example are listed below.

1. Create DAO classes
2. Create a data value object (DVO) class
3. Configure the datasource and MyBatis-specific classes in an application context file
4. Create a MyBatis-specific "sqlMapConfig.xml" file
5. Create a MyBatis-specific "mapper.xml" file
6. Create a main class to test the code

The preceding steps are described in the following sections:

Step 1: Create DAO classes.

The `PetDAO` interface contains methods used for executing the SQL statements. The complete class code is provided below.

```java
// PetDAO.java
package com.learning.db.mybatis.velocity;

import java.util.List;

public interface PetDAO {

    public PetDVO getPetObject(String petName);

    public PetDVO getPetObjectData(String petName, String sex);

    public List<PetDVO> getAllPets(List<PetDVO> petList);

    public List<PetDVO> getMatchingPets(List<String> petNamesList);

    public List<PetDVO> findAllSnakes();

    public void createPet(PetDVO petDVO);

    public void updatePetData(PetDVO petDVO);

}
```

The `PetDAOImpl` class implements the above specified methods. The complete class code is provided below. This class contains methods used for executing various select statements.

```java
// PetDAOImpl.java
package com.learning.db.mybatis.velocity;

import org.mybatis.spring.SqlSessionTemplate;
import java.util.*;

public class PetDAOImpl implements PetDAO {

    private SqlSessionTemplate sqlSessionTemplate;

    public PetDVO getPetObject(String petName) {
        HashMap<String, String> inputMap =
                        new HashMap<String, String>();
        inputMap.put("name", petName);
        inputMap.put("sex", "f");
        return sqlSessionTemplate.selectOne("getPetObject", inputMap);
    }

    public PetDVO getPetObjectData(String petName, String sex) {
        HashMap<String, String> inputMap =
                        new HashMap<String, String>();
        inputMap.put("name", petName);
        inputMap.put("sex", sex);
        return sqlSessionTemplate.selectOne("getPetObjectData",
                            inputMap);
    }

    public List<PetDVO> getAllPets(List<PetDVO> petList) {
        HashMap<String, List<PetDVO>> inputMap =
                        new HashMap<String, List<PetDVO>>();
        inputMap.put("petList", petList);

        return sqlSessionTemplate.selectList("getAllPets", inputMap);
    }

    public List<PetDVO> getMatchingPets(List<String> petNamesList) {
        HashMap<String, List<String>> inputMap =
                        new HashMap<String, List<String>>();
        inputMap.put("namesList", petNamesList);

        return sqlSessionTemplate.selectList("getMatchingPets",
                            inputMap);
    }

    public List<PetDVO> findAllSnakes() {
        HashMap<String, String> inputMap =
                        new HashMap<String, String>();
        inputMap.put("species", "snake");
        inputMap.put("sex", "m");
        inputMap.put("owner", "Den");

        return sqlSessionTemplate.selectList("findAllSnakes",
                            inputMap);
    }
```

```java
    public void createPet(PetDVO petDVO) {
        HashMap<String, Object> inputMap =
                        new HashMap<String, Object>();
        inputMap.put("name", petDVO.getName());
        inputMap.put("owner", petDVO.getOwner() );
        inputMap.put("species", petDVO.getSpecies() );
        inputMap.put("sex", petDVO.getSex());
        inputMap.put("birth", petDVO.getBirth());
        inputMap.put("death", petDVO.getDeath());

        sqlSessionTemplate.insert("createPet", inputMap);
    }

    public void updatePetData(PetDVO petDVO) {
        HashMap<String, Object> inputMap =
                        new HashMap<String, Object>();
        inputMap.put("birth", petDVO.getBirth());
        inputMap.put("sex", petDVO.getSex());
        inputMap.put("name", petDVO.getName());

        sqlSessionTemplate.update("updatePetData", inputMap);
    }

    public void setSqlSessionTemplate(SqlSessionTemplate
                sqlSessionTemplate) {
        this.sqlSessionTemplate = sqlSessionTemplate;
    }
}
```

Step 2: Create a data value object class

The following data value object maps the table data. The "pet" table column values are mapped to the PetDVO class attributes.

```java
// PetDVO.java
package com.learning.spring.db;

import java.util.Date;
import java.io.Serializable;

public class PetDVO implements Serializable {

    private String name;
    private String owner;
    private String species;
    private String sex;
    private Date birth;
    private Date death;

    // Add getter and setter methods
}
```

Step 3: Configure the datasource and MyBatis-specific classes in an application context file

The spring application context file is used to configure the datasource, MyBatis session factory, MyBatis template, and data access objects. The complete application context XML file is provided below and is named the "applicationContext-mybatis-velocity.xml".

```xml
<?xml version="1.0" encoding="UTF-8"?>
<!DOCTYPE beans PUBLIC "-//SPRING//DTD BEAN//EN"
         "http://www.springframework.org/dtd/spring-beans.dtd">
<beans>

     <!-- Configure datasource -->
     <bean id="dataSource"
         class="org.springframework.jdbc.datasource.
                                DriverManagerDataSource">
         <property name="driverClassName">
             <value>com.mysql.jdbc.Driver</value>
         </property>
         <property name="url">
             <value>jdbc:mysql://localhost:3306/test</value>
         </property>
         <property name="username">
             <value>root</value>
         </property>
         <property name="password">
             <value>mysql</value>
         </property>
     </bean>

     <!-- Configure session factory and load myBatis configurations -->
     <bean id="sqlSessionFactory"
         class="org.mybatis.spring.SqlSessionFactoryBean">
         <property name="dataSource" ref="dataSource"/>
         <property name="configLocation"
                 value="sqlMapConfigVelocity.xml" />
     </bean>

     <!-- Configure MyBatis DB template -->
     <bean id="sqlSessionTemplate"
         class="org.mybatis.spring.SqlSessionTemplate">
         <constructor-arg index="0" ref="sqlSessionFactory"/>
     </bean>

     <!-- Configure DAO classes -->
     <bean id="petDAOImpl"
             class="com.learning.db.mybatis.velocity.PetDAOImpl">
         <property name="sqlSessionTemplate" ref="sqlSessionTemplate"/>
     </bean>

</beans>
```

Step 4: Create a MyBatis-specific "sqlMapConfigVelocity.xml" file

This file contains database-specific settings, domain object configurations and mapper files. The complete XML file is provided below and is named the "sqlMapConfigVelocity.xml".

```xml
<?xml version="1.0" encoding="UTF-8" ?>
<!DOCTYPE configuration PUBLIC "-//mybatis.org//DTD Config 3.0//EN"
```

```
            "http://mybatis.org/dtd/mybatis-3-config.dtd">

<configuration>

    <settings>
        <setting name="cacheEnabled" value="true"/>
        <setting name="lazyLoadingEnabled" value="true"/>
        <setting name="multipleResultSetsEnabled" value="true"/>
        <setting name="useColumnLabel" value="true"/>
        <setting name="useGeneratedKeys" value="false"/>
        <setting name="defaultExecutorType" value="SIMPLE"/>
        <setting name="defaultStatementTimeout" value="100"/>
        <setting name="defaultScriptingLanguage" value="velocity"/>
    </settings>

    <!-- Configure domain objects -->
    <typeAliases>
        <typeAlias alias="PetDVO"
                type="com.learning.db.mybatis.velocity.PetDVO"/>
        <typeAlias alias="velocity"
                type="org.mybatis.scripting.velocity.Driver"/>
    </typeAliases>

    <!-- Configure mapper XML files -->
    <mappers>
        <mapper resource="petmappervelocity.xml"/>
    </mappers>

</configuration>
```

Step 5: Create a MyBatis-specific "petmappervelocity.xml" file

This file contains database-specific SQL statements such as select, insert, delete, and update. The complete mapper XML file is provided below and is named the "petmappervelocity.xml"

```
<?xml version="1.0" encoding="UTF-8" ?>
<!DOCTYPE mapper PUBLIC "-//mybatis.org//DTD Mapper 3.0//EN"
            "http://mybatis.org/dtd/mybatis-3-mapper.dtd">

<mapper namespace="com.learning.db.mybatis.velocity">

    <select id="getPetObject" lang="velocity"
            parameterType="java.util.Map" resultType="PetDVO">
        SELECT ID as id, NAME as name, OWNER as owner,
            SPECIES as species, SEX as sex,
            BIRTH as birth, DEATH as death
        FROM Pet where name = @{name, jdbcType=VARCHAR}
    </select>

    <select id="getPetObjectData" lang="velocity"
            parameterType="java.util.Map" resultType="PetDVO">
        SELECT ID as id, NAME as name, OWNER as owner,
            SPECIES as species, SEX as sex,
            BIRTH as birth, DEATH as death
        FROM Pet where name = @{name, jdbcType=VARCHAR}
        AND sex = @{sex, jdbcType=VARCHAR}
```

```
        </select>

        <select id="getAllPets" lang="velocity"
            parameterType="java.util.Map" resultType="PetDVO">
            SELECT * from Pet
            #where()
                #repeat($_parameter.petList $petObj "," " name IN (" ")")
                    @{petObj.name}
                #end
            #end
        </select>

        <select id="getMatchingPets" lang="velocity"
                parameterType="java.util.List" resultType="PetDVO">
            SELECT * from Pet
            #where()
                #in($_parameter.namesList $item "name")
                    @{item}
                #end
            #end
        </select>

        <select id="findAllSnakes" lang="velocity"
                parameterType="java.util.Map" resultType="PetDVO">
            #set($sex = $_parameter.sex )
            #set($owner = $_parameter.owner + '%')

            SELECT * FROM Pet WHERE species = @{species, jdbcType=VARCHAR}
            #if($!sex)
                AND sex =  @{sex, jdbcType=VARCHAR}
            #end

            #if($!owner)
                AND owner LIKE @{owner, jdbcType=VARCHAR}
            #end
        </select>

</mapper>
```

Let us review the sample SQL statement.

- select → used for executing the select statements
- lang → this attribute specifies the scripting language
- getPetObjectData → represents the unique name used for identifying the SQL statement.
- resultType → represents the ResultSet return type mapping object.
- parameterType → represents the type of input parameter.
- NAME, OWNER etc. → represents the database table column names.
- name, owner, etc. (column alias names) → represents the domain object properties

MyBatis maps the database's returned ResultSet to the domain objects. The Java code used to retrieve all pets is provided below.

```
HashMap<String, String> inputMap = new HashMap<String, String>();
inputMap.put("name", petName);
inputMap.put("sex", sex);
```

```
PetDVO petDVO =sqlSessionTemplate.selectOne("getPetObjectData",inputMap);
```

Step 6: Create a main class to test the code.

Listing 6-1 provides the complete class code; run the following stand-alone class to view the output on console.

Listing 6-1: Stand-alone class to test the MyBatis DAO methods with velocity scripting

```java
// MyBatisMain.java
package com.learning.db.mybatis.velocity;

import org.springframework.context.support.
                    ClassPathXmlApplicationContext;
import org.springframework.context.ApplicationContext;
import java.util.*;

public class VelocityMain {

    public static void main(final String[] args) throws Exception {
        ApplicationContext context =
            new ClassPathXmlApplicationContext(
            new String[]{"applicationContext-mybatis-velocity.xml"});

        VelocityMain main = new VelocityMain();

        // Calling private methods
        main.getPetObject(context);
    }

    private void getPetObject(ApplicationContext context) {
        PetDAO petDAO = (PetDAO) context.getBean("petDAOImpl");
        PetDVO petDVO = petDAO.getPetObject("Slimmy");
        System.out.println("--- PetDVO ---" + petDVO);
    }

    private void getPetObjectData(ApplicationContext context) {
        PetDAO petDAO = (PetDAO) context.getBean("petDAOImpl");
        PetDVO petDVO = petDAO.getPetObjectData("Slimmy", "m");
        System.out.println("--- PetDVO ---" + petDVO);
    }

    private void getAllPets(ApplicationContext context) {
        PetDAO petDAO = (PetDAO) context.getBean("petDAOImpl");
        List<PetDVO> petList = new ArrayList<PetDVO>();

        PetDVO petDVO = new PetDVO();
        petDVO.setName("Slimmmy");
        petList.add(petDVO);

        PetDVO petDVO1 = new PetDVO();
        petDVO1.setName("Slim");
        petList.add(petDVO1);

        List<PetDVO> petListOutput = petDAO.getAllPets(petList);
        System.out.println("--- petListOutput ---" +
```

```
                        petListOutput.size());
}

    private void getMatchingPets(ApplicationContext context) {
        PetDAO petDAO = (PetDAO) context.getBean("petDAOImpl");
        List<String> namesList = new ArrayList<String>();
        namesList.add("Slimmmy");
        namesList.add("Slim21");

        List<PetDVO> matchingPets = petDAO.getMatchingPets(namesList);
        System.out.println("--- matchingPets ---" +
                            matchingPets.size());
    }

    private void findAllSnakes(ApplicationContext context) {
        PetDAO petDAO = (PetDAO) context.getBean("petDAOImpl");
        List<PetDVO> petList = petDAO.findAllSnakes();
        System.out.println("--- petList ---" + petList.size());
    }
}
```

Example 2: Inserting the Data – Insert Operations

Add the following method to the `PetDAO` interface and its implementation class. This example is used to "insert" a new record into the "pet" table.

```
public void createPet(PetDVO petDVO) {
    HashMap<String, Object> inputMap = new HashMap<String, Object>();
    inputMap.put("name", petDVO.getName());
    inputMap.put("owner", petDVO.getOwner());
    inputMap.put("species", petDVO.getSpecies());
    inputMap.put("sex", petDVO.getSex());
    inputMap.put("birth", petDVO.getBirth());
    inputMap.put("death", petDVO.getDeath());

    sqlSessionTemplate.insert("createPet", inputMap);
}
```

The corresponding select statement in the "mapper.xml" file is provided below.

```
<insert id="createPet" lang="velocity" parameterType="java.util.Map">
    <selectKey keyProperty="id" resultType="int" order="BEFORE">
        SELECT PET_ID_SEQ.nextval AS id FROM dual
    </selectKey>

    INSERT INTO Pet (ID, NAME, OWNER, SPECIES, SEX, BIRTH)
    VALUES (@{id}, @{name}, @{owner}, @{species}, @{sex}, @{birth})
</insert>
```

The following examples illustrate the use of the `SqlSessionTemplate` class for executing update statements.

Example 3: Updating the Data – Update Operations

Add the following method to the `PetDAO` interface and its implementation class. This example is used to "update" an existing record in the "pet" table.

```
public void updatePetData(PetDVO petDVO) {
    HashMap<String, Object> inputMap = new HashMap<String, Object>();
    inputMap.put("birth", petDVO.getBirth());
    inputMap.put("sex", petDVO.getSex());
    inputMap.put("name", petDVO.getName());

    sqlSessionTemplate.update("updatePetData", inputMap);
}
```

The corresponding select statement in the "mapper.xml" file is provided below.

```
<update id="updatePetData" lang="velocity" parameterType="java.util.Map">
    UPDATE Pet p
    SET p.birth = @{birth},
        p.sex = @{sex}
    WHERE p.name = @{name}
</update>
```

The following examples illustrate the use of the `SqlSessionTemplate` class for executing delete statements.

Example 4: Deleting the Data – Delete Operations

Add the following method to the `PetDAO` interface and its implementation class. This example is used to "delete" an existing record in the "pet" table.

```
public void deletePet(PetDVO petDVO) {
    HashMap<String, String> inputMap = new HashMap<String, String>();
    inputMap.put("species", petDVO.getSpecies());
    inputMap.put("name", petDVO.getName());

    sqlSessionTemplate.update("deletePet", inputMap);
}
```

The corresponding select statement in the "mapper.xml" file is provided below.

```
<delete id="deletePet" parameterType="java.util.Map">
    DELETE FROM Pet WHERE name = @{name} AND species = @{species}
</delete>
```

Summary

This section summarizes the features provided by the MyBatis-Velocity framework for executing SQL statements. Figure 6-1 summarizes the most important points described in this chapter.

- MyBatis-Velocity provides "`#if`", "`#repeat`", "`#foreach`", "`#where`", and "`#set`" statements for building the dynamic SQL statements.
- Configure the `defaultScriptingLanguage` attribute value to "velocity" in your MyBatis configuration file to make use of the MyBatis-velocity features.
- Configure the scripting language driver alias in your MyBatis configuration file.

Figure 6-1 Executing SQL statements using MyBatis-Velocity.

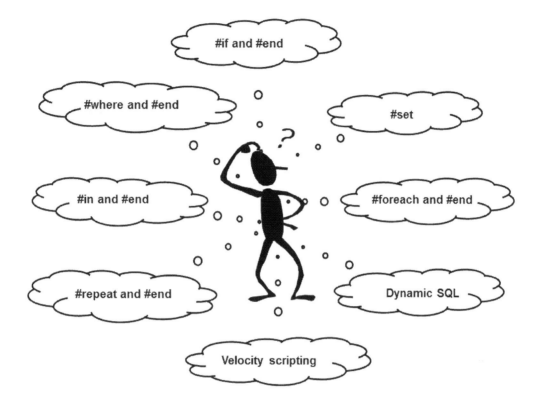

Chapter 7. Migration from iBatis to MyBatis

MyBatis is completely redesigned from its existing iBatis framework. The newly redesigned MyBatis framework is not backward compatible with its existing iBatis framework. This chapter illustrates the migration from iBatis-2.0 to MyBatis-3.0.

This chapter will discuss the following topics:

- Migrating from iBatis to MyBatis.
- MyBatis support for logging information.

Migrating from iBatis to MyBatis

This section illustrates the migration from iBatis-2.0 to MyBatis-3.0.

iBatis to MyBatis

This section illustrates the required changes for converting iBatis to MyBatis. The required changes are listed below.

- Upgrade the JAR files
- Update the SQL mapper XML file
- Update the SQL map configuration file

The following list of JAR files are used in iBatis-2.0

- ibatis-common-2.jar
- ibatis-sqlmap-2.jar

The following list of JAR files are used in MyBatis-3.0

- mybatis-3.2.2.jar

The following "sqlMapConfig.xml" file is used in iBatis-2.0

```xml
<?xml version="1.0" encoding="UTF-8" ?>
<!DOCTYPE sqlMapConfig PUBLIC "-//iBATIS.com//DTD SQL Map Config 2.0//EN"
            "http://www.ibatis.com/dtd/sql-map-config-2.dtd">

<sqlMapConfig>
    <settings
        cacheModelsEnabled="true"
        enhancementEnabled="true"
        lazyLoadingEnabled="true"
        maxRequests="128"
```

```
            maxSessions="10"
            maxTransactions="5"
    />

    <!-- List all SQL mapper files here -->
    <sqlMap resource="student.xml"/>

</sqlMapConfig>
```

Similarly, the equivalent "sqlMapConfig.xml" file used in MyBatis-3.0 is provided below.

```
<?xml version="1.0" encoding="UTF-8" ?>
<!DOCTYPE configuration PUBLIC "-//mybatis.org//DTD Config 3.0//EN"
            "http://mybatis.org/dtd/mybatis-3-config.dtd">

<configuration>

    <settings>
        <setting name="cacheEnabled" value="true"/>
        <setting name="lazyLoadingEnabled" value="true"/>
        <setting name="multipleResultSetsEnabled" value="true"/>
        <setting name="useColumnLabel" value="true"/>
        <setting name="useGeneratedKeys" value="false"/>
        <setting name="defaultExecutorType" value="SIMPLE"/>
        <setting name="defaultStatementTimeout" value="100"/>
    </settings>

    <!-- List all domain objects here -->
    <typeAliases>
        <typeAlias alias="PetDVO"
                type="com.learning.db.mybatis.PetDVO"/>
        <typeAlias alias="User" type="com.learning.db.mybatis.User"/>
    </typeAliases>

    <!-- List all SQL mapper files here -->
    <mappers>
        <mapper resource="petmapper.xml"/>
    </mappers>

</configuration>
```

The following "petmapper.xml" file is used in iBatis-2.0

```
<?xml version="1.0" encoding="UTF-8" ?>
<!DOCTYPE sqlMap PUBLIC "-//iBATIS.com//DTD SQL Map 2.0//EN"
            "http://www.ibatis.com/dtd/sql-map-2.dtd">

<!-- Place filename in namespace field value without extension (.xml) -->
<sqlMap namespace="student">

    <!-- List all domain objects here -->
    <typeAlias alias="Student" type="com.pearson.ibatisdemo.Student"/>

    <select id="getStudentById"
        parameterClass="java.lang.Integer" resultClass="Student">
        select id as id, first_name as firstName, last_name as lastName
```

```xml
    from student where id = #id#
</select>

<!-- Returns all records -->
<select id="getAllStudents" resultClass="Student">
    select id as id, first_name as firstName, last_name as lastName
    from student
</select>

<!-- Returns set of students -->
<select id="getSetOfStudentsList"
        parameterClass="java.util.Map" resultClass="Student">
    select id as id, first_name as firstName, last_name as lastName
    from student
    where first_name = #firstName#
</select>

<!-- Returns all records with multiple input parameters -->
<select id="getStudentsBasedOnConditions"
    parameterClass="java.util.Map" resultClass="Student">
    select * from student
    where id = #id#
    and first_name = #firstName#
</select>

<!-- Returns set of records -->
<select id="getSetOfStudents" resultClass="Student">
    select id as id, first_name as firstName, last_name as lastName
    from student
</select>

<!-- Returns a map contains Single Object.
                Not like Java Map concept -->
<select id="getStudentsMap" parameterClass="java.lang.Integer"
                    resultClass="java.util.HashMap">
    select id as id, first_name as firstName, last_name as lastName
    from student where id = #id#
</select>

<!-- Insert using inline parameters -->
<insert id="insertStudentRecord"
        parameterClass="com.pearson.ibatisdemo.Student">
    insert into student (id, first_name, last_name)
    values (#id#,#firstName#,#lastName#)
</insert>

<!-- Insert using externally defined parameter map -->
<parameterMap id="externalStudentParameterMap"
            class="com.pearson.ibatisdemo.Student">
    <parameter property="id" jdbcType="NUMBER"/>
    <parameter property="firstName" jdbcType="VARCHAR"/>
    <parameter property="lastName" jdbcType="VARCHAR"/>
</parameterMap>

<insert id="insertStudentRecordUsingParamMap"
        parameterMap="externalStudentParameterMap">
    insert into student (id, first_name, last_name)
```

```
        values (?, ?, ?)
    </insert>

    <!-- Update using inline parameters -->
    <update id="updateStudentRecord" parameterClass="java.util.Map">
        update student set first_name = #firstName#
        where id = #id#
    </update>

    <!-- Update using external map. Order is mandatory -->
    <parameterMap id="updateParamMap"  class="java.util.Map">
        <parameter property="lastName" jdbcType="VARCHAR"/>
        <parameter property="id" jdbcType="NUMBER"/>
    </parameterMap>

    <update id="updateUsingParamMap"  parameterMap="updateParamMap">
        update student set last_name = ? where id = ?
    </update>

    <!-- Delete using inline parameters -->
    <delete id="deleteStudent" parameterClass="java.util.Map">
        DELETE from student WHERE id=#id#
    </delete>

</sqlMap>
```

The following "petmapper.xml" file is used in MyBatis-3.0

Here, refer to the "petmapper.xml" file provided in Chapter-2. The following section illustrates the required changes in XML files.

The following notation is used to specify inline parameters in iBatis-2.0

```
#firstName#
```

The following notation is used to specify inline parameters in MyBatis-3.0

```
#{firstName}
```

The following document type definition used in iBatis-2.0.

```
<!DOCTYPE sqlMap PUBLIC "-//iBATIS.com//DTD SQL Map 2.0//EN"
        "http://www.ibatis.com/dtd/sql-map-2.dtd">
```

The following document type definition used in MyBatis-3.0.

```
<!DOCTYPE configuration PUBLIC "-//mybatis.org//DTD Config 3.0//EN"
        "http://mybatis.org/dtd/mybatis-3-config.dtd">
```

The following root element is used in iBatis-2.0.

```
<sqlMapConfig>
```

The following root element is used in MyBatis-3.0.

```
<configuration>
```

The following XML element is used in iBatis-2.0 to list the SQL mapping files.

```
<sqlMap resource="petmapper.xml"/>
```

The following XML element is used in MyBatis-3.0 to list the SQL mapping files.

```
<mappers>
    <mapper resource="petmapper.xml"/>
</mappers>
```

The following XML element is used in iBatis-2.0. The `<typeAlias>` XML element is defined in SQL mapper file.

```
<typeAlias alias="Pet" type="com.learning.database.PetDVO"/>
```

The following XML element is used in MyBatis-3.0. The `<typeAlias>` XML element is moved to MyBatis configuration file.

```
<?xml version="1.0" encoding="UTF-8" ?>
<!DOCTYPE configuration PUBLIC "-//mybatis.org//DTD Config 3.0//EN"
"http://mybatis.org/dtd/mybatis-3-config.dtd">

<configuration>
    ...

    <typeAliases>
        <typeAlias alias="PetDVO"
                type="com.learning.db.mybatis.PetDVO"/>
    </typeAliases>

<configuration/>
```


iBatis-Spring to MyBatis-Spring

The following list of JAR files are used in MyBatis-Spring.

- mybatis-spring-1.2.0

iBatis-2.0: Spring provides `SqlMapClientTemplate` class for executing SQL statements in iBatis-2.0. The complete application context XML file is provided below and is named the "applicationContext-ibatis2.xml".

```
<?xml version="1.0" encoding="UTF-8"?>
<!DOCTYPE beans PUBLIC "-//SPRING//DTD BEAN//EN"
        "http://www.springframework.org/dtd/spring-beans.dtd">
<beans>

    <bean id="dataSource"
        class="org.springframework.jdbc.datasource.
                        DriverManagerDataSource">
```

```xml
        <property name="driverClassName">
            <value>oracle.jdbc.OracleDriver</value>
        </property>
        <property name="url">
            <value>jdbc:oracle:thin:@localhost:1521:xe</value>
        </property>
        <property name="username">
            <value>SPOWNER</value>
        </property>
        <property name="password">
            <value>PASSWORD</value>
        </property>
    </bean>

    <bean id="sqlMapClient"
        class="org.springframework.orm.ibatis.SqlMapClientFactoryBean">
        <property name="configLocation">
            <value>sqlMapConfig.xml</value>
        </property>
    </bean>

    <!-- iBatis DB template -->
    <bean id="sqlMapClientTemplate"
        class="org.springframework.orm.ibatis.SqlMapClientTemplate">
        <property name="sqlMapClient">
            <ref bean="sqlMapClient"/>
        </property>
        <property name="dataSource">
            <ref bean="mySqlDataSource"/>
        </property>
    </bean>

    <!-- DAO class -->
    <bean id="petDAOImpl" class="com.learning.db.mybatis.PetDAOImpl">
        <property name="sqlMapClientTemplate">
            <ref local="sqlMapClientTemplate"/>
        </property>
    </bean>
</beans>
```

MyBatis: MyBatis-Spring provides `SqlSessionTemplate` class for executing SQL statements. The complete application context XML file is provided below and is named the "applicationContext-mybatis.xml".

```xml
<?xml version="1.0" encoding="UTF-8"?>
<!DOCTYPE beans PUBLIC "-//SPRING//DTD BEAN//EN"
        "http://www.springframework.org/dtd/spring-beans.dtd">
<beans>

    <!-- Configure datasource -->
    <bean id="dataSource"
        class="org.springframework.jdbc.datasource.
                            DriverManagerDataSource">
        <property name="driverClassName">
            <value>com.mysql.jdbc.Driver</value>
        </property>
```

```xml
        <property name="url">
            <value>jdbc:mysql://localhost:3306/test</value>
        </property>
        <property name="username">
            <value>root</value>
        </property>
        <property name="password">
            <value>mysql</value>
        </property>
    </bean>

    <!-- Configure session factory and load MyBatis configurations -->
    <bean id="sqlSessionFactory"
        class="org.mybatis.spring.SqlSessionFactoryBean">
        <property name="dataSource" ref="dataSource"/>
        <property name="configLocation" value="sqlMapConfig.xml" />
    </bean>

    <!-- Configure MyBatis DB template -->
    <bean id="sqlSessionTemplate"
        class="org.mybatis.spring.SqlSessionTemplate">
        <constructor-arg index="0" ref="sqlSessionFactory"/>
    </bean>

    <!-- DAO class -->
    <bean id="petDAOImpl" class="com.learning.db.mybatis.PetDAOImpl">
        <property name="sqlMapClientTemplate">
            <ref local="sqlMapClientTemplate"/>
        </property>
    </bean>
</beans>
```

Logging

MyBatis can use several logging frameworks such as Log4J, JDK Logging, Apache Commons Logging, and so forth. These frameworks can be used to log the information while executing the SQL statements.

The following statement enables the Log4J logging.

```
org.apache.ibatis.logging.LogFactory.useLog4JLogging();
```

The following statement enables the JDK logging.

```
org.apache.ibatis.logging.LogFactory.useJdkLogging();
```

The following statement enables the Apache Commons logging.

```
org.apache.ibatis.logging.LogFactory.useCommonsLogging();
```

Similarly, the following statement enables the console logging.

```
org.apache.ibatis.logging.LogFactory.useStdOutLogging();
```

This section illustrates the complete use of Log4J framework.

The "log4j.peroperties" file is used to specify the logging level. The complete "log4j.peroperties" file is provided below.

```
log4j.rootCategory=mybatis,stdout
# Console output...
log4j.appender.stdout=org.apache.log4j.ConsoleAppender
log4j.appender.stdout.layout=org.apache.log4j.PatternLayout
log4j.appender.stdout.layout.ConversionPattern=%5p [%t] - %m%n

# MyBatis logging configuration...
log4j.logger.com.learning.db.mybatis.core.CoreMyBatisMain=INFO
```

The following method uses Log4J to log the messages on the console.

```
public List<PetDVO> selectPets(String sex) throws Exception {
    HashMap<String, String> inputMap = new HashMap<String, String>();
    inputMap.put("sex", sex);

    // Enable the logging
    org.apache.ibatis.logging.LogFactory.useLog4JLogging();
    return getSqlSession().selectList("selectPets", inputMap);
}
```

Use any suitable logging framework; all provide the same functionality. Before running the application, make sure "log4j.properties" file is available in your classpath. Run the above method to view the output on console. An example output is provided below.

```
DEBUG [main] - Logging initialized using 'class
org.apache.ibatis.logging.commons.JakartaCommonsLoggingImpl' adapter.
DEBUG [main] - Logging initialized using 'class
org.apache.ibatis.logging.log4j.Log4jImpl' adapter.
DEBUG [main] - PooledDataSource forcefully closed/removed all
connections.
DEBUG [main] - PooledDataSource forcefully closed/removed all
connections.
DEBUG [main] - PooledDataSource forcefully closed/removed all
connections.
DEBUG [main] - PooledDataSource forcefully closed/removed all
connections.
DEBUG [main] - Opening JDBC Connection
DEBUG [main] - Created connection 457572055.
DEBUG [main] - ooo Using Connection
[oracle.jdbc.driver.T4CConnection@1b45fed7]
DEBUG [main] - ==>  Preparing: SELECT ID as id, NAME as name, OWNER as
owner, SPECIES as species, SEX as sex, BIRTH as birth, DEATH as death
FROM Pet where sex = ?
DEBUG [main] - ==> Parameters: m(String)
```

References

The below given documents and web links are referenced in this book.

MySQL Database - http://www.mysql.com/

Oracle database express edition
http://www.oracle.com/technetwork/products/express-edition/downloads/index.html

Spring Transaction Management
http://static.springsource.org/spring/docs/2.0.x/reference/transaction.html

AOP with Spring - http://static.springsource.org/spring/docs/2.0.8/reference/aop.html

ORM Data Access with Spring - http://static.springsource.org/spring/docs/2.5.x/reference/orm.html

Distributed transaction using Spring
http://www.javaworld.com/javaworld/jw-01-2009/jw-01-spring-transactions.html

MySQL installation for Windows7
http://www.landpro.com.au/Windows_7_Install_MySQL.php

MyBatis-Spring module
http://www.mybatis.org/spring/getting-started.html

MyBatis SQL maps with Spring
http://static.springsource.org/spring/docs/3.0.0.M4/reference/html/ch13s06.html

MyBatis with Spring - http://www.mybatis.org/spring/

Apache velocity - http://velocity.apache.org/

MyBatis and Velocity - http://mybatis.github.io/velocity-scripting/

MyBatis JAR files - http://code.google.com/p/mybatis/downloads/list

Spring-JDBC
http://static.springsource.org/spring/docs/3.0.x/spring-framework-reference/html/jdbc.html

Hibernate - http://www.hibernate.org/

Spring XML Schema configurations
http://static.springsource.org/spring/docs/2.5.3/reference/xsd-config.html

Spring projects - http://www.springsource.org/projects

Index

Made in the USA
Lexington, KY
22 June 2015